Echoes of Narcissus

in the

Gardens of Delight

Jo Robinson

Editor: Eleanor Visser

Chapter One

Donna tried not to look at Marco blatantly flirting with his accountant at the buffet table. Her eyes kept darting in that direction anyway. The woman's hand flitted from his shoulder to his chest, eyes sparkling as she smiled up at him. It had been a long time since his cheating had hurt much, but it still made her angry. She barely managed to prevent a sneer of revulsion. Her husband was the best looking man in the room. Very tall, with his Italian Irish heritage bestowing fine chiselled features, glossy black hair, and clear blue eyes. Even so, just looking at him these days often made her feel nauseous. She knew now that beneath that polished shell of beauty and charm, lay a vicious, manipulative, greedy entity that could barely be called human.

Marco had never raised his hands to her, but he knew just how to inflict maximum pain in other ways. And he had done so consistently for three decades. She had hurt in ways that most people would never understand. The mental agony of a breakdown a few years back had morphed into odd physical illnesses, but she'd firmly believed that these were all because of her own imperfection. She'd believed that she was mentally unstable, possibly bipolar, and that her own inherent craziness was the reason for her outrageous feelings of hopelessness and despair, and the times, the many times, that she had been completely filled with nameless, reasonless terror for days on end. Apart from her almost constant underlying anxiety, she'd got over those terrible months when she'd so totally fallen apart. She'd meditated and looked inward. Prayed to a God that she hadn't believed in. Finally she'd managed to build a wall around her heart, she'd lowered her expectations to nothing, and so she managed to get through her days mostly uninjured.

But she never forgot the trauma of that time. Those memories remained, even though she remembered very little else. Marco managed to start an argument almost daily, with his condescending, disrespectful insults, his lies and cheating, and his little tricks. Too many years of that and she'd just simply broken. She'd grown fearful. Fearful of walking outside in the forest. Fearful of being alone. Fearful of people. Fearful of the dark. Fearful of summer storms. Fearful of everything. She'd turned to him then, hoping for kindness. For help. But she'd been ignored. Apart from looks of disdainful disgust, Marco wasn't interested in what she was going through. She'd trembled constantly, and jumped at the slightest noise. She couldn't even sign her own signature on the till slips in the supermarket without shaking. Then he would ask loudly, laughingly, making sure that everyone heard, "Why are you shaking so much?" She used to be mortified when people stared at her like some drunk or crazy woman.

Then one day the fear stayed. All the time. She had constantly remained in a state of utter dread and alarm. Physically she'd hurt from the tension in her body that never went away. Thoughts raced through her mind constantly. It went on for months, and then, when she could take no more of being so broken, she forced herself to look for some source of relief. Trying to find the source of her madness. She'd realised then that she would have to look within for help, unaware back then that what was happening to her was being purposefully done by Marco, but fully aware that he wouldn't help her. She imagined that her insanity had been brought on by karma, by all the bad things that she had done over the course of her life, and by the loss of God. And so she'd purposefully remembered all that she had done wrong, every tiny little hurt she'd ever inflicted, or imagined that she'd inflicted, and magnified them in her mind to the point where her past actions cut her heart like knives, as she purposely relived the pain that whoever she thought that she had hurt must have felt. And she was sorry. Deeply sorry for each imagined thing.

She'd reached out to any higher power that might possibly be watching. She'd never been to church in her life, or read a bible, so even then, when she finally had reached out, she hadn't expected anything to happen, because she really hadn't believed.

But something had happened. Suddenly she found a small strength growing. Enough strength to venture out again, and she saw the wilderness with a new clarity. In everything she looked at, she seemed to see the love of the divine. And so, slowly, she clawed her way out of her brokenness, her lonely abyss. Nature had saved her. Plants and the soil had stopped her losing her sanity entirely. She'd known deep down, even back then, that Marco had broken her, but always pushed that thought aside, choosing rather to believe that at the end of everything she was mad, flawed, and it was who she was that had caused him to treat her the way that he had. To stop loving her.

The strength she had felt pour into her heart, when the love she had either imagined or been real, had been enough for her to do the only thing that she could to stop spiralling further down. She had stopped allowing his actions to hurt her. Mostly. She was still highly strung. Still had attacks of terror, but they were manageable. As her mind and soul had slowly erected barriers to deflect anything that could take her back to that pit of helpless pain, it had begun to dawn on Donna that there was something more than a little wrong with her husband. She'd realised very quickly after they'd married that even though he chose mostly to portray himself as a kind, helpful, and capable man, he could be rude and persistently goading to the point where strangers had actually punched him a few times. She'd always wondered at his nastiness, wondered why he always taunted and disrespected people who he considered weaker than himself. But even so, when that meanness had been directed at her, he'd always managed to twist things around, convincing her that it was her own fault.

She'd lied, often, to cover up the results of some of the things he had done, and she'd always made huge efforts to portray an idyllic marriage to anyone who had briefly come into their lives, although people seldom stayed. They had no friends. He had acquaintances from work, but no friends. All of these things had stewed in her mind without making any connections. Marco consistently managed to create some drama or unpleasant distraction every single day, and until her breakdown she had never really had any time to consider much more than his daily inflicted mental torture. After she'd picked up the pieces of herself, and resolved that she would sink no deeper, she'd made time to think. She closed her heart off and would not allow any of his jibes to hit home again. And against all odds, she had begun to heal and gather strength.

Then, so recently that she was still reeling from the enormity of it, the reason that she had suffered so long appeared out of nowhere one day, and smacked her right between the eyes with the force of a revivalist preacher's forehead shove. She wasn't crazy at all. *He was.* Marco McGee was a certifiable narcissist. Psycho. Psychopathic. Psychotic. Malignant. Donna didn't care which word was used, but the day that that fact had dawned on her with crystal clear clarity, was the day she swore that he wouldn't get to hurt her at all any more, one way or another. She needed to get as far away from him as she possibly could. She just had to figure out how. She was furious, but calm. She felt nothing but contempt for him now. Nobody knew what he'd done to her. She'd hidden it all, always ashamed, feeling that there must be something deeply flawed within herself. Always believing that the loss of his love was because of her. Always longing for that love to return, and for him to notice her again. Always trying to figure out where she had gone wrong. Of *course* it must have been something that she had done wrong. She hadn't realised that he'd never loved her at all.

Donna had very little access to the world outside her home, and the technology in it was limited to an ancient television set that she seldom watched. She preferred for her own vivid imagination to immerse her into the world of books instead. If it wasn't for the fact that one of the few pleasures she had to call her own was her garden, she might never have found out. She could have gone to her grave believing that the barren, painful landscape of her marriage had been caused by her. She'd only mentioned once that it would be nice to connect to her daughter every day on Facebook if she could have a computer, but Marco had laughed and said that he wasn't wasting money just so that she could spend her already useless days messing around online. It occurred to her then that even if he had allowed it, nothing she said to Shelley would be safe from his eyes anyway, and that would just lead to more ammunition for him to throw at her whenever he felt like it. No. Facebook would be a very bad idea. Marco had never given her any privacy, and respected no boundaries. He rummaged through her wardrobe, dug in her handbag, scrolled through her phone. Not that there was ever anything to see there. He took her things whenever he wanted them, never to be seen again, simply denying all knowledge if she ever asked. Or he'd break something, replace it broken as it was, and look at her as is she was completely off her head when she mentioned it. He still tried to occupy all of her space, creating constant chaos and discord in her small world.

In the beginning, when she was totally immersed in loving him, she'd found that appealing, thinking that it was because he felt the same way as she did. Thinking that it was love making him want to be as close as he could to her. *Stupid. Stupid.* It had always all been about control with him. But Marco had a strong aversion to soil and dirt. He seemed almost afraid of it, and the only time he would venture outside was when he was surrounded by his fawning work lackeys on the tiled patio. The garden beyond that, and what lay beyond the garden still, had always been only for Donna. Her love, her secret, and her sanctuary. Her obsession.

She'd desperately wanted heirloom tomato seeds. Living at the edge of miles and miles of wild mountainous wilderness, quite a way away from the quaint, but not very well-stocked little town of Wilson Springs, meant that she would have to search for them farther afield, but she had no excuse to give Marco for her to go anywhere other than her usual shops. She called her daughter, and asked her to try and find some on the internet, but Shelley was up to her ears with work and life. She seldom came home at all anymore. She'd moved out as soon as she could, as far away as she could too it seemed to Donna, and regardless of Marco's sneering that she would amount to nothing, and come snivelling back when she crashed and burned, she'd built up a thriving business with her handcrafted jewellery. Her father's attempts to make her work for him had failed miserably, and his sneering derision of her creative ways had only made her despise him more.

She insisted that her mother dig out her old laptop from the wardrobe in her room and look online herself. It had never occurred to Donna that she could operate, let alone enjoy owning a computer. She'd been surprised at how quickly she'd learned how to use it, and even more surprised at the pleasure she got from the worlds she found behind that small screen. She'd been tucking it back away in Shelley's wardrobe when Marco was home, knowing that seeing her using it would either elicit anger or scorn from him, and those things always meant her losing something she enjoyed. She'd given up all of her once loved hobbies and activities through the years because of Marco's mocking contempt. She saw now how he had stolen her freedom. The freedom to dance. To listen to the music she loved, or wear the clothes she liked. In the end she did none of these things rather than endure his mockery and insults. So she hid the little computer well.

While she was familiarising herself with the laptop, clicking on all the icons already there, she came across Shelley's eBook library. This in turn led her to an online site which did indeed stock heirloom tomato seeds. The wide variety available, and the cost of them made her hesitate. She couldn't buy them all, no matter how much she wanted to, so she would need to take her time and choose just a few. As she sat and thought, idly clicking through the books on sale while she was there, she was suddenly presented with a book on psychotic behaviour, narcissist personality disorder in particular, nestled in between two books revealing the secrets of growing championship daffodils. About to move on, shaking her head at the oddness of this new virtual world, the blurb beneath the cover had caught her eye. *That was her.* That was how she felt. She'd believed that she'd been suffering with mental instability for years in one form or another, and Marco had never failed to confirm his firm belief in this also, every time she succumbed to depression or random attacks of anxiety or panic. So she'd bought the book, and three hours later sat stunned, feeling like she'd been run over by a herd of bison. The book described her life, blow by blow, as if it had been written about her. Her life with Marco.

She sat for hours, alternating between frantically going from website to website, reading the experiences of others in the thrall of a narcissist, and staring out of the window remembering incidences both huge and small, almost exactly the same as those she was reading about in many cases, during the course of her marriage. These things had made no sense to her before. Now they did. The way Marco had cleverly twisted everything to make it look like she was always at fault in arguments that had confused her with their seeming pointlessness. Now, looking back, they were so obviously purposely started by him so that he could have an excuse to go away for a while, or to punish her for some perceived disobedience. Leave her alone and afraid while he completely ignored her for weeks. As if she didn't exist, and wasn't worth being acknowledged as a person. And then the carefully calculated kindnesses that he occasionally blessed her with, and which she always received with fawning gratitude, regardless of her confusion. She could now see that these gifts weren't given with any affection, but rather with the desire to be worshipped or to impose guilt. It had all been about control. He'd owned her mind and body for thirty years. Then there had been those surreal times when Marco had blatantly taken all credit for something she had done or suggested around the house when he was showing off to some random guest. Things that had seemed silly at the time, but had definitely been more fodder for her to doubt her own sanity.

One adamant piece of advice given to all those living with these psychopaths, was to get away from them immediately, and cut all ties. To never have any contact with them ever again. Oh, how badly she wanted to do that. But as Donna raged inwardly for days, thinking of ways to do this, all the while watching Marco's every move, and having all his words confirm what she now knew, she realised that actually doing this might be easier said than done in her case. Vengeful thoughts, confused thoughts, and thoughts of doubt vied for her attention. She was furious with the man who now appeared to have intentionally tortured her for most of her adult life, and more furious with herself for allowing him to do it.

Racing thoughts of where she'd live, and how she'd earn a living filled her with terror, because she knew that if she left, Marco would make sure that she did so with nothing. She was fifty five years old, had no work skills or experience, and hardly any social skills either, not to mention several recurring ailments that sometimes almost flattened her. She had lost contact with all of her sparse and already scattered family shortly after she'd married. Marco had seen to that, she now realised. All she knew about his family was that they were estranged. He refused to discuss any of them, and she'd never met them. Her friends had all been lost along with her hobbies and any opportunity of employment. They never went out together unless he wanted to show her off to work clients, and the few times she had tried to join a conversation, he would say something that would make her look like an idiot. Every time. So she'd learned to shut her mouth in company.

Suddenly she realised how successful he'd been in making her believe that she was unattractive, and lucky that he married her. Now she saw that that wasn't true at all. He'd *wasted* her. Wasted her as a living, loving, human being. He'd wasted her life, because he wasn't human. Not human in the way that she understood human to be. The simplicity of what she hadn't been able to see, because she could never have imagined anyone being that way, stunned her. She'd managed to control her anger these past few weeks, and she was sure that Marco had no idea of the turmoil in her. He also had no clue that she now knew what he was, and that that knowledge alone had completely changed her. She wondered if *he* had any idea what he was. Memories of her life before him, her life with him, and small glimpses of who she really was, the self that she'd managed to bury over the years, came frequently now. She let them come without saying a word to him, or taking the terrifying step of walking out of the door for one final time.

She decided to wait a while instead. Wait and see if she could settle the chaos in her mind, and possibly find a way out that wouldn't bring on the extremely vindictive wrath of Marco McGee. She knew that she should leave right now, just as all those who knew these people said she should, but she found that after her initial rage, she vacillated between hating him and wondering if maybe she was wrong. Maybe she was the narcissist in her marriage. The psycho. Had it really been her mental issues that had caused all that had happened? She also pondered the fact that Marco had settled down over the past few years after her breakdown. She'd thought that it was because he was trying to be kind to her after her breakdown because he finally felt sorry for her, but now she wondered if it was just because he was satisfied that he'd broken her. The days of screaming fights were in the past. As time had gone on, she'd retreated more and more into herself, and that occasionally attracted his interest, which meant more attempts at charm. Outwardly their life looked peaceful, and would seem like a normal, happy marriage to an outsider. But there was no love here. No affection at all. As the days went by she realised that she felt dead inside. The only love she felt was for her daughter, her garden, and her secret.

Her secret loves. Those were the only things that could make her heart briefly soar.

Then doubt would be replaced by fury once again. He had made her this way. He had chipped away at her confidence, her joy, and her spirit until they were gone. Totally gone, and now she couldn't care about very much at all. Even if she left him now, she wondered if she could ever care again. Ever love again. She doubted it, and so she stayed. Why uproot herself and try and begin her life again at such a ripe age, when it seemed to already be over? She had created a beautiful home over the years. She was used to her solitude, and she was used to the numbness that had replaced seldom remembered feelings of joy. She would stay for now, until she knew that if she did leave, it could not possibly happen on his terms. Her hatred of Marco grew, no matter how hard she tried to stop it. Every remembered injury, and there had been so many, made her despise him more each day, but still she waited, fear of the known and the unknown vying constantly for her attention. She was terrified that she'd explode, reveal her new knowledge of him, and lay herself wide open to the consequences. With him there were always consequences.

"Can I top up your glass for you Mrs McGee?"

Donna, snapped abruptly from her reverie, and looked up into the round, pink cheeked, smiling face of a woman gripping a weighty looking tray of wine bottles. She breathed in deeply and blinked.

"Thank you," she said, holding out her glass, trying to put a name to the face. "Are you new here?"

"No. I'm the caterer tonight." The woman replaced the bottle on the tray, fished a business card from a pocket in her capacious skirt, and handed it over. Her gaze flicked knowingly between Donna and Marco, whose arm was now strung casually around the slender waist of his latest conquest. When she looked back at Donna she was tight-lipped, but she had an oddly engaging glint in her eye.

"Call me," she said. "Call me anytime."

Donna inspected the card in her hand, almost tossing it in the ashtray on the little table beside her, but then putting it in her bag instead, not wanting to hurt the woman's feelings if she found it there later.

Elvira Young. Caterer, psychic, and landscaper. For all your sustenance needs, edible, spiritual, and physical, CALL 087 136-3000

She watched her, Elvira, blithely weaving her way through Marco's staff and clients, offering drinks left and right, wondering who'd hired her. Marco most certainly wouldn't have if he'd seen this card, having no time for people he referred to as arty type whack jobs, and Elvira with her flowing hippie print skirt and bright blue tints in her long brown hair would fit that description perfectly in his estimation. Finally, when the guests began to say their goodbyes and leave, she put down her glass and made her way over to the buffet table. Marco looked at her briefly but continued his animated discussion with a small group of clients, making no attempt to remove his hand from his accountant's rump.

She frowned a little, trying to remember the woman's name, and caught her husband's fleeting smile when he saw it. He must have taken it for jealousy. He had always revelled in her jealousy. *Idiot*. Quickly turning aside to hide her flaming cheeks, she was met with the vision of a cascade of the most beautiful heirloom tomatoes she had ever seen, glistening plumply in the middle of the mostly empty trays of canapés. These were what she wanted! Shades of red, yellow, green and plum, in all sizes and shapes flowed from an upturned Roman urn on the centre of the table. A search for Elvira revealed that the caterer had already left, but she managed to sneak a few of those shining beauties into her handbag before she left, in the hope that she could grow them herself from the seeds.

Chapter Two

"Watching paint dry would be more productive than playing with rotten tomatoes," said Marco.

Donna didn't turn to face him, continuing instead with throwing the tomato pulp sticking to the newspaper she'd spread them on to dry the seeds, and the barren trays of soil into a large bin bag, disappointed that her attempts to germinate the heirlooms had failed.

He walked around in front of her, always needing to be seen. Looked at. Admired.

"What are we having for dinner?"

"Fish," she replied shortly, keeping her eyes on her destination as she headed off to her shed, all the way behind her rose garden, where he never went.

Her loathing of him had grown these past weeks, her thoughts firmly focused on remembering and dissecting all the things that had happened over the years to turn her into the miserable shell she'd become.

Things that she had always taken the blame for. The more she delved and dug, and realised that each and every one of them had not only not been her fault, but rather done to her with planning and malicious intent, the more she hated the one who was responsible. She couldn't bear to look at him now, and his constant physical placements of himself in her line of vision made her realise that her new reactions to him could be dangerous.

In the past couple of days, he seemed to have figured out that something had changed in her, and this was clearly confusing him. So he'd been trying very hard to charm her again. Coming home on time, and focusing totally on her. A mere few months ago Donna would have fallen for his tricks as she always had. But not this time. And she was far too angry to pretend.

"Fish and what?"

His voice behind her startled her, and she spun around, shocked that he had followed her here after decades of refusing to set foot beyond the patio. He was smiling down at her, that old loving expression firmly in place.

"Pardon?" she asked.

"I said what are we having with the fish." He reached over and took the garbage bag from her hand. "Here. Let me help you with this."

He walked off in the direction of Donna's shed, treading carefully on the grass he hated so much, confident that she would follow.

But she couldn't. No matter how ingrained in her it was to do what he wanted to keep the peace, to avoid the anger, and the days of silence. Those frigid days where he made sure she knew that without him she would always be alone. Lonely. Nothing. She shook herself and turned abruptly back to the house.

She was chopping kale when he came back in and took a beer out of the fridge.

"Can I pour you something?" he asked, coming up behind her, putting his hand casually on her elbow, and with seeming affection softly running his fingers up to her shoulder.

She froze. Marco hadn't touched her in a very long time, and she knew very well that she repulsed him. He certainly repulsed her. They had stopped touching in any way after years of him trying to get her to have sex with him in ways that prostitutes would hesitate to do, to try and entice his limp member into action. Always horrible, demeaning things. When she'd furiously refused, disgusted and insulted that he'd assumed she'd ever even consider such things, he never argued or raged about what was due to him. In fact he'd seemed relieved, and he'd never made any further attempt to get close to her in any way. Not so much as the touch of his finger, or a peck on the cheek had come her way for many, many years. Now that she saw him for what he was, she realised what he was doing. He wanted the old meek Donna back. Not this one who ignored him and refused to acknowledge his greatness with so much as the slightest glance. He was bringing out the big guns that had always worked before. Her flesh prickled beneath his hand. She carefully placed her knife on the board and moved away from him.

"No thanks," she replied brightly, "It's a bit early for me."

She smiled hearing the surprised intake of breath at the implied insult, waiting for the sarcastic or angry comeback without her usual trembling. None came. She looked at him in passing as she headed out the door to collect some fresh herbs. His face looked pale, and slightly afraid. She wasn't though. For the very first time since she could remember she wasn't anxious, she wasn't tense, and her mind was totally clear. She didn't give a damn how Marco felt, whatever he was capable of feeling, and right now she didn't give a damn what he would do either. She planned to do exactly what she chose until she could untangle the wasted decades of her life with him. She would do it in her own time, and on her own terms, but she would have to try much harder to give him no further inkling of what was really going on inside her. The fact that he considered her stupid and incapable of thinking for herself might just work in her favour for a change.

Snipping off a long stem of plump Romano tomatoes growing in the midst of a large patch of thyme, her thoughts went back to her failed crop of heirlooms, and she wondered if she still had Elvira's card in her bag. She had a few hundred dollars stashed away, that she had saved little by little from the regulated amounts of housekeeping money given to her once a week, so she could easily buy a small selection if the woman was prepared to sell some.

Marco was in his study with the door closed. She paused outside a while, listening to the drone of his voice. His was probably whining about his bitch of a wife to his new lover. *Jackie*. That was her name. Donna found Elvira's card buried beneath a wad of toilet paper in her bag, and stared at it nervously for a while. She never phoned strangers. In fact she never phoned anyone except Shelley and very occasionally Marco when she absolutely had no choice. She took her cell phone to the very end of her garden, squared her shoulders and tapped the numbers. The opulent scent of the huge bank of petunias behind her calmed her, and she breathed in deeply while she waited for the ringing to stop.

"Hello."

"Hello," she said awkwardly, "I'm looking for Elvira Young."

"This is she," came the laughing response.

"Yes," said Donna. "I was wondering—. This is Donna McGee. I was wondering about your tomatoes."

"My tomatoes?"

"Yes.   From the function.   The heirloom tomatoes. Were they not from you?"

"*Oh*. Of course, yes. I see now. The table arrangement. Yes, yes. I grow them myself. They're a sight to behold when they're all in fruit."

"Would you be interested in selling a few seedlings?" asked Donna. "Or viable seeds."

"Of course my dear. In fact you're welcome to have as many as you'd like right now, with pleasure. I've planted much more than I can hope to sell this season.   When would you like to come around? Tomorrow?"

And so it was done. Elvira sent her address straight away, and Donna had an appointment to see her the next day at ten. It was her shopping day, so Marco wouldn't need to be told. He was lying on the couch looking grim, and ignored her when she told him that supper was ready, so she went and sat on the patio with a glass and a bottle of wine, marvelling that the only thing she felt at his soundless aggression was irritation. Not the way she had felt for so long when he decided to exclude her in silence. That old feeling of being an unwelcome stranger in her own home, when she would go and sit quietly somewhere that he wasn't, and try to ignore that particular deep ache in her body that came from muscles tensed too tight, for nebulous hard to understand reasons, for far too long. *Bastard*. Donna sipped her wine, inhaled the delightful scents of her magical garden, and dived back into her memories. Memories of who she had been. Who she really was. The real Donna. Beneath this damaged woman she had become concealed, but she was clawing her way to the surface now, in spite of being buried so deeply.

Chapter Three

She found the smallholding easily. Elvira met her in the large car park in front of her house, dressed in bright pink dungarees, wellington boots, and an immense moth-ridden garden hat.

"Welcome Mrs McGee,' she said, enfolding Donna's outstretched hand in both of her warm, wet, soil encrusted ones, before wiping them down on the front of her pants.

"Sorry," she said laughing, "I really should wear gloves. Come in. Come in. We'll have a cup of tea before you choose your tomatoes. I have some wonderful chillies too. Good healthy seedlings you might like also. And fuchsias. Brand new varieties. Do you like to garden Mrs McGee?"

Donna trotted to keep up, taking in the spectacle that was Elvira's front garden. The scent of healthy damp earth and flowers filled the air, and they tumbled from pots and outrageous containers from the roof of the house to the floor in a profusion of all the hues and colours of the rainbow.

"Yes," she murmured. "Yes. I like to garden."

Elvira led the way through a bright red front door, down the wide cluttered passage to her kitchen. The old farmhouse was large, but there wasn't a bare corner to be seen. Ornaments and trinkets vied for space with bags of potting soil, pot plant containers, and plants in various stages of growth. A large sleeping dog of no instantly identifiable breed briefly opened an eye, and then went back to sleep, warmly surrounded by several squirming kittens. A group of ducks waddled hastily out when the pair came in to the room.

Donna sat stiffly, trying unsuccessfully to relax her shoulders and unclench her hands. She looked around while her hostess made tea, and sliced thick chunks from a warm gingerbread loaf, without enquiring if any was wanted. The counters were covered with racks of cooling pies and pastries, and the savoury smells mingled comfortably with the scent of the flowers and shrubs that wafted through the door on a warm breeze.

Elvira settled into the chair right beside her. Donna wasn't at ease with people in close proximity to her these days, but the calm warmth that exuded from her hostess was somehow deeply comforting, so she smiled and had a bite of ginger loaf instead of doing what she usually did, and moving away.

"I'll have to take these to the shop in a minute." Elvira nodded at the cooling pastries. "They don't last long."

"Shop?" Donna quailed at the thought of either having to wait alone in a stranger's kitchen or having to trail along with her, feeling like a spare part.

"My little coffee shop. It's just around the back. On the way to the seed beds anyway. I originally planned on doing my readings there, but somehow it evolved when my clients became my friends, and kept demanding coffee and cake instead of having their futures told," Elvira chuckled, reaching over suddenly and squeezing her hand. "You won't mind carrying a couple of pies for me will you?"

What a very *tactile* person. Donna stared at the hand that gripped hers so tightly for a few seconds before yanking it away. Elvira's grin remained firmly in place, and her eyes twinkled knowingly as she finished her tea and started packing baked goods into baskets.

"I'm always amazed at how much people like to eat these things," she said, jiggling a quiche on its way to the basket that she passed over, and then headed for the door. "We're a funny old bunch, us humans, with the things we think we need. Or the things we really don't need, but so believe we do."

Donna silently followed her out, still feeling the imprint of that hand on hers. She knew that it had meant nothing. A simple friendly gesture. People touched each other all the time in friendship. It was normal. The difference was that she hadn't felt the touch of a friend, or anyone at all, in a very long time. She liked Elvira. The down to earth honesty and warmth that she projected. A tiny spark of excitement grew at the thought of having a friend again. Someone to laugh with, and confide in. The spark faded quickly though. The woman was just selling her some seedlings. She probably had her own life filled with others already. Good people. Normal people. Normal people didn't hang around Donna for very long. Marco had long ago perfected the art of making her look like a fool when she'd tentatively tried to make a friend. He did that or else he came on to them, which either chased them away, or they became another notch in his long belt of lovers.

She sighed, and then suddenly stopped in her tracks, reverie broken at the sight of the garden around her. The cobbled path she stood on meandered onwards to a small trellised building. A few tatty sofas and chairs scattered outside beneath the roses entwined in the trellis were filled with people, and the soft murmur of their conversations filtered through the cascading shrubbery. Apart from a small, immaculate piece of lawn on the other side of the shop, every other available piece of the huge, walled space was filled with flowers of every imaginable colour and description.

Peeping through the foliage here and there, were dainty wrought iron chairs, and beautifully made statuettes of mythical creatures. A small waterfall cascaded over the wings of a dragon perched on a hippy peace sign made of brass. The terraced pools beneath it shimmered in the sun, surrounded by dancing, fairy-like fuchsia blossoms, with violets at their feet. Her heart lurched at the crazy beauty of the scene, and made her think of her secret. The thing that she'd begun so many years ago that had become her obsession. Probably the thing that had saved her sanity, and the only thing that she would miss more than anything if she ever managed to leave her husband.

"You like my little garden then, Mrs McGee?"

She tore her gaze away from the magic around her. "Yes. I—. Donna. Call me Donna."

Elvira nodded. "Come on then," she said. "Let's go get you some seedlings."

She followed her into the coffee shop, nodding as she moved through the seated patrons. Every one of them greeted her with effusive smiles, as if she were a welcome part of their little group, and then went back to their conversations. A few were tapping away at laptops, and one woman was reading a book, feet tucked up under her as if she was in her own home, with a half-eaten cream scone balanced on her knee.

Trying not to stare, and wanting more than anything to stay, she trotted to keep up with Elvira as she headed through a tiny kitchen filled with urns and piles of multicoloured antique crockery, and then out the back door. They moved through a formal herb garden surrounded by a topiary of sweet bay, fringed lavender, and lemon verbena, and ducked under the eaves above a tiny entrance in the wall. Marching into the distance were rows and rows of seedlings and also a row of hothouses. Such things should be mundane, but to Donna even they were imbued with magic. This whole place seemed to be. Elvira handed her a broad wicker basket from a pile leaning against the wall, and took one herself. By the time they got to the seedlings, she felt a little more like herself again, and not like Alice in Wonderland.

"How many heirlooms do you have in mind? Do you have beds, or are you planning to go with containers?"

"Beds," she replied. "I've just prepared some new ones in the grounds behind my flower garden. Quite large beds actually. But I'm not only putting tomatoes in them. So, just as many as you can spare. It's a huge property actually, and unused, mostly—. I—."

Elvira nodded, not smiling for the first time since they'd met, she looked shrewdly into Donna's eyes.

"Good, good," she said. "It's good that you're using it. It's always such a shame when beauty lies fallow and unloved."

She turned away and started collecting seed trays and popping them into the basket, while Donna wondered if she'd been wrong in construing that sentence to have more than one meaning. She frowned.

Such nonsense she'd been imagining these past few weeks. This woman knew nothing about her at all.

"Now, this one's a real gem. Cherokee Chocolate." She stopped suddenly and looked up. "I tell you what. If you have such big beds ready, why don't I pop by and have a look? To get a better idea of how many you need. Then I can drop everything off in my truck instead of trying to squeeze them into your car. We'll just have a wander round now and you can take some other bits with you instead."

The thought of Marco seeing loads of seedlings and plants being delivered made her blood run cold. Being the CEO of his own company, he did what he liked, and arrived home at all hours under one pretext or another. He liked to catch her off guard, and even though he appeared to make more than enough of it, he never liked her spending money on herself. This had always been obvious, and although his ways were subtle on that subject, they were effective. Seeing her buy a slightly more expensive deodorant than she usually did would earn her at the very least a raised brow or a derisive grunt, and the definite notion implied that she didn't deserve nice things. As far as he knew she never had any money at all, and he'd made it abundantly clear that he didn't want anyone in her life other than himself. The slightest notion that anyone was interested in being her friend always brought out his devil. She could just imagine his rudeness if he ever met Elvira. She would be mortified, and never be able to come back here again. That's one thing she knew now. She definitely wanted to come back here again.

"No. No. I'll get them a few at a time. If that's alright with you. No need for you to go to any trouble."

Elvira looked her directly in the eye.

"Why?"

"Why?" repeated Donna.

"Yes. Why? It will be no trouble at all, and besides," she smiled. "There's nothing I enjoy more than sticking my nose into other people's gardens."

After listening to a few senseless reasons for her not to visit, and not at all put off by the distance out of town she would have to drive to get there, Elvira shook her head firmly, and said, "It makes sense to have all the seedlings there for when you start planting, and these little guys are ready to be planted right now. Let's have a quick coffee, then I'll follow you home, and drop off what you need tomorrow. Bob's your uncle!"

What started out as a never to be repeated hour of putting Elvira off from coming to her house, sipping coffee and chatting to strangers, became instead a firm longing in Donna to stay, and to come again, and again. She was comfortable here. Maybe it was the surroundings, but she felt it was more than that. It felt like she was amongst people who she'd known for years. Kindred spirits. Elvira refused to charge her a cent for the few fuchsias and rosebushes she'd picked out, insisting that she was doing her a favour by thinning out her glut, and refused to have her mind changed about going to inspect Donna's beds. Donna decided that it would be safe after all. Marco seldom came home on her shopping days, and now that she thought about it, lately he'd seemed very distracted and spent a lot more time than usual away from home.

After introductions had been made, she found out that most of the guests in the coffee shop were regulars. All very enthusiastic gardeners. Rabid lovers of plants, every one of them and mostly firm friends, rather than acquaintances. A few of them came in most days, and spent hours there doing the work that paid their bills. Artists and creative types mostly. Darkly handsome Laurence was a website developer. Saul with the grey beard and the sad, sad eyes was a painter. The woman reading a book, Sandy, turned out to be a writer of fiction, and Donna was enthralled listening to her talk about her latest novel. She was delighted to find herself smiling and laughing with them, totally relaxed. When they asked her about herself, she deftly turned the conversation back to them, and they moved on without being offended by her unwillingness to talk about herself. She had nothing interesting or honestly pleasant to say about her life, and for once the thought of her usual lies about her happy home and husband never even tried to surface. She couldn't lie to these people. A strange sensation had begun to grow now. A sensation so long not felt that it almost hurt. She felt a sense of belonging with these newly met friends. A small sense of entitlement to be human again blossomed, and with it the notion that not everyone she came across saw her as the mentally unstable, stupid, boring housewife with nothing to offer, that Marco had over the years finally almost convinced her that she was.

Chapter Four

Elvira had been effusive in her praise as they strolled through Donna's garden. She knew that it was just as beautiful as Elvira's magical creation, only in a much bigger, and more formal way. She had taken thirty years to make it so after all. It felt good to finally share this with another human being, but the other—. Sharing that had never been part of her plan, and even now a little voice inside her was screaming at her to turn back. But then the excitement of finally sharing her secret joy with another got the better of her. Elvira would never meet Marco anyway.

"We're alike, you and I," said Elvira as she strode up the narrow gravel path in between blooming banks of thorny, creeping red roses on the steep incline at the official end of the garden. "This is nothing short of a work of art. Wouldn't like to trip and fall over here though."

Donna smiled at her. This thorny wall was just another one of the subtle barriers she had created to ensure that Marco stayed away. After the shock of his trip to her shed, she hoped that he never would take notice of this almost hidden little path, and use it to find out what she'd been doing. If he ever did, she knew that would be the crushing of the last piece of herself that she had managed to keep.

"My husband isn't fond of the wilderness," she said. "He didn't like the view when we first moved here. That's why I had the terraces made. You can't miss the peaks in the distance, but they totally block the valley from sight at the house."

"Didn't like the view?" Elvira laughed. "That's the oddest thing I've heard in a long while. Why not move to town then? There are all those old mansions that would fit perfectly with your standing in the community. It would make for a much shorter commute to your factory anyway."

Donna couldn't prevent a snort. She didn't give a damn about status, and Marco had made it perfectly clear that it was *his* factory. *His* money. She owned nothing, and never would if he had anything to do with it. She knew now that the only reason for living here for so long had been another ploy to separate her from society and the possibility of connecting with anyone other than himself. He liked her isolated with only himself in her universe.

"He's not home during the day much." She stopped and turned to look back as she reached the top of the embankment. "And I love it here. I'm used to the quiet, and I wouldn't like to lose this beauty now."

Elvira caught her breath, then stood slack-jawed, staring out at the vista beneath her. The manmade terrace angled steeply down to the flat plain below that stretched to the foot of the forest and the mountains. A winding concrete stairway flanked by a broad ramp and sturdy banisters was the only way down. The property's original farmhouse and outbuildings nestled in the tree line, surrounded by an ancient low stone wall. An entire farm, hidden away from view. The old bright red tractor that Marco had forgotten he'd bought when they were first married, when he was still pretending to be smitten with the same things that Donna was, peeped from the barn where she had parked it after ploughing and preparing her new vegetable field below.

They followed the steps down in silence, Elvira switching between looking at the amazing sight beneath her, and staring hard at the back of Donna's head.

"How long ago did you build these terraces?" she asked.

"Almost thirty years," replied Donna, stepping off the final stair and onto the wild grass below.

"But—. But you say your husband doesn't—."

"He never comes here. Never goes much further than the patio. Marco doesn't remember this place." Donna suddenly stopped in her tracks, the full realisation of the risk she was taking by bringing this woman here finally sinking in. "I don't want him—. I don't want him to remember this place."

Elvira frowned and shook her head. "I won't tell anyone." Then she grinned and squeezed Donna's arm. "Come on then. I can't wait to explore your secret farm."

Slightly out of breath from the long walk from the stairway to the old farm gates, she inspected the results of the years of Donna's work. The orchard, filled with fruit-bearing trees of so many varieties in blossom or fruit was a colourful, heavenly scented work of art. The prolific exotic blooms and fruits planted and painstakingly cared for in the greenhouse, all burgeoning with health and vitality told of years of dedicated care and love.

"Cuttings," she breathed, gazing in disbelief at the neatly labelled foreign herbs and plants in the medicinal garden. "I must have cuttings. Where on Earth did you get these?"

"Stolen mostly." Donna pinched a dead leaf off her barley sugar plant, an original native of South Africa as she recalled. "We were allowed—. My daughter has always attended a boarding school. Every time I fetched her, or dropped her off I used to visit the botanical gardens. And other places sometimes too.

It's amazing the plants people have growing against their fences. I've found some really exotic species that way."

"Stolen?" Elvira looked very slightly shocked for a second, and then burst out laughing. "I *love* it," she said. "Although I don't think I would have the balls to swipe cuttings from the botanical gardens."

Donna blushed, although she didn't feel bad about her forays into thievery when it came to her gardens. Plants should be for everyone. She followed the exclaiming and gesturing woman around for an hour, amazed at how comfortable she felt with her. Elvira wanted to see every nook and cranny of the huge green world Donna had created. There was no formality here, only wild beauty on a scale way too huge to believe that it had been created by one woman. Finally, after making a note of the size of the beds allocated to heirloom tomatoes and chillies, she turned and walked purposefully towards the old farmhouse.

"No! Please." Donna tried to steer her back towards the terrace in the distance, terrified of having her real secret revealed. A secret that someone as honest and nice as her guest was highly unlikely to approve of. "There's not much to see there."

Elvira stopped abruptly, and turned to look deeply into her eyes. The obvious concern and compassion in her face made Donna's stomach lurch. She had to turn her face away.

"Maybe some other day then," said Elvira gently. "Maybe some other day."

By the time they'd crossed the terrace, and were sipping their tea in the sunroom, Elvira was back to chatting away, as if she hadn't seen the alarm brought on by her move towards the old farmhouse, but now her bright eyes took in every twitch and squirm as her hostesses' eyes constantly flitted to the window overlooking the drive.

"I've only been running my little place for a couple of years now," she said. "But what you've made down there is nothing short of miraculous. Like a whole other world. It's a shame that nobody gets to share such splendour. Does anyone else go there?"

"Never. No one but me."

"And me now."

Donna dragged her eyes away from the window. As the day drew to a close, the thought of the possibility of Marco walking in on them was making her feel ill. She stood quicker than she should have, and nearly fell back down.

"Yes. I have to—. I must—."

"That's alright dear," said Elvira, getting up just as hastily and moving towards the door, looking at her watch. "I'm sure you have dinner to prepare. Things to do."

Standing by her truck in the drive, Donna could barely stop herself from pushing her into the cab.

"Why don't you pop over to the coffee shop tomorrow before I come out with the plants? I've had a few ideas for your tomato garden while we were walking around down there, and we can add a few rare varieties into the mix. They all deserve a place there."

Donna shook her head wildly. She couldn't go there again. She'd already done too much. *Shown too much.* She wished she'd never laid eyes on an heirloom tomato now. Now Elvira would see her true self. That rude person who could never be part of anything.

"No. No."

Elvira's eyes widened at the sight of the panicked woman in front of her, who now couldn't seem to tear her gaze from the meandering country road at the bottom of the drive. Then she grimaced, squared her jaw, and nodded. Grasping Donna's elbow, she asked.

"Which day then?" she asked. "Which day would be good for you?"

"I can't."

"Why? I know you liked it. You liked everyone, and they all liked you."

Finding it impossible to dislodge her elbow from that grip, Donna knew that if she didn't agree, any minute now Marco's black Bentley would appear, and all her secrets would be revealed. And then she would be in a world of trouble. She didn't have to go anywhere no matter what she said now.

"Monday," she said. "I'll come on Monday next week. It's my shopping day."

Suddenly Elvira was all about speed. She jumped in her truck, and pulled hurriedly out the drive.

"Good," she yelled out of the window. "I'll be around tomorrow anyway to drop the first lot off. And if we don't see you Monday, I'll come and fetch you."

Chapter Five

Her fear of being caught with a visitor of her own had been unfounded. Marco hadn't come home at all that night. As always, he hadn't phoned or sent a message. Punishment for her behaviour she realised. For not letting him have her full and undivided attention. He knew how much she hurt when he did these things. Used to hurt. He couldn't know that she didn't anymore. She used to worry that he'd been injured or killed in an accident, and build herself up into panic attacks imagining all the terrible things that could have happened to him. Whenever he'd come home and find her like that, desperately worried and anxious at his absence, he'd laughed and called her a silly little woman, and overly clingy.

After she'd found out about his first affair, then she'd worried about who he was with. Those he'd always flat out deny, and tolerate no conversation on the subject. Marco didn't give a damn about evidence, and he'd never really tried to conceal his cheating. Sometimes it seemed as though he wanted her to know. She always used to spend nights like this in tears, afraid, sure that she'd finally lost him forever, and wishing she knew what she had done wrong to make it so. This time, after she'd gotten over her panic at the thought of him bumping into Elvira, she'd made herself a large bowl of guacamole, opened a king size bag of cheddar chips, poured herself a glass of wine, and happily watched a romantic movie on television instead, very happy not to have Marco's tangibly disturbing aura in the house with her. She wondered about her uncharacteristic choice of movie genre, and the odd feeling of peace and serenity that filled her without him in her space. It was strange not to feel frightened and worried.

She'd nodded off, and awoke with the answer front and centre in her mind. The reason that she had made a point of not seeing love and romance for the majority of her adult life was because if she didn't look at it, she could believe that it didn't exist in any other form than the one she believed she had. Her sudden and complete understanding so recently of the thing that her husband really was had changed her in ways she was only beginning to understand. She had chosen not to see love to save herself the pain of realising that she had none in her life. Deep down she must have always known that he didn't love her, but she had gone on pretending that he did.

She knew that she wasn't stupid, and she found it difficult to accept that she had been so manipulated for so long and so badly that she could feel the damage to her psyche. To her mind and her body. Filled with regret at the barren toxic wasteland she saw when she looked back over the years of her marriage, she kept asking herself how she could have changed it. Made it better, or left. She honestly couldn't see how. By the time she'd figured out that there was something wrong it had been too late to leave. He'd promised her early on that if she left, she'd never see Shelley again, and she'd believed him. Trapped in Marco's crazy hamster wheel, groomed, and constantly feeling mentally unbalanced, how could she have left then? Now she was beginning to think that she could leave, because she understood what had happened, and he couldn't take her daughter from her now. She was all grown up. Unbelievable as his actions had been over the years, now that she knew what he had done to her, all those feelings of being unhinged were gone with the knowledge that all along it had been his own madness that he had successfully, and intentionally, projected on to her.

"Poor thing," she muttered to her previous self.

She bustled around preparing for Elvira's arrival. Marco wouldn't come home today. None of his disappearances had ever lasted for less than a couple of days at least. Smiling and humming at the feeling of freedom this thought brought, she decided that she would use this time to have fun. Have fun and maybe spoil herself a little. It was alright that Marco would be picturing her curled up on the sofa, hair unbrushed, and face swollen up like an overripe tomato from all the crying. She didn't care. She hadn't felt this happy and in control for years.

*

"So," said Elvira, as they put the last of the seedling trays in one of the greenhouses. "What's behind the old house? I'd love to take a little stroll in those woods—." She paused at the look on Donna's face. "Sometime. It would be nice to have a look around there sometime."

"It's not safe right now," said Donna. "Bears. And wild—. Wild things. They come down for the fruit. And there's nowhere to hide back there." Donna had never seen any wild thing around the farm larger than a squirrel, but her own lie came across so well that she found herself nervously peering into the tree line.

"There's nowhere to hide here either," said Elvira, looking over her shoulder sharply.

"We'll go for a walk soon," said Donna. "There's a shotgun in the safe up at the house. We'll take that along for safety. Although I'm not supposed to know—."

Elvira's pace as they headed towards the terraces was distinctly faster than it had been on arrival, but she slowed a little when she saw her hostesses' beetroot complexion. Donna was trying not to laugh. Both of their reactions to her fib suddenly seemed eye-wateringly funny.

"What aren't you supposed to know dear?"

Donna took several deep breaths before replying. "The combination to the gun safe. Marco isn't comfortable with me knowing it. You know. In case someone breaks in and ends up shooting me with it."

When she'd mentioned that gun, she'd remembered the day when she had seen an odd selection of numbers written on a scrap of paper tucked into his father's old pocket watch. She'd wanted to polish it, but instead had headed off to the safe and tried the combination. It had worked. She'd wished it hadn't when she'd opened that door though, to be confronted with not only the shotgun, but piles of the most disgusting pornography, along with strange looking items of rubber clothing. She hadn't wanted to even contemplate what Marco got up to with those things.

Elvira frowned. "Seems pretty dumb to have a gun in the house without you knowing how to get at it. At least then if someone did break in, you would have a chance of defending yourself. Your husband sounds like rather an—. Interesting fellow."

Donna laughed as they walked into the kitchen. "Yes," she said, "He most certainly is." She turned to smile at the flushed face beside her. "Would you like a coffee?"

"I have to get back now. Got a shipment of manure due in an hour. What a shame that you can't come into town till Monday. We always have a couple of sundowners as the afternoons fade, and chat about whatever comes up. Sometimes I do readings. You really should let me do one for you soon. I suppose your husband wouldn't be impressed with you rolling in after dark reeking of margaritas. Such a pity."

Donna stared at her. Why shouldn't she go? She knew very well why she shouldn't go. What was good for the gander was most definitely not good for the goose in her marriage. If Marco ever found out she'd been having drinks with a group of single men and women, she'd be out on the street in the blink of an eye is why she shouldn't go. She trembled slightly at the thought. But still, the notion of going out, talking to pleasant, clever people, and just being allowed to be herself raised her heart rate as well as the corners of her mouth. Why not? He would never find out. She certainly wasn't going to tell him, and the coffee shop was well away from the haunts of his cronies.

"I *will* come," she said to a startled Elvira, who'd been washing her hands in the sink. "I'll just change out of these garden things, and then I'll come through."

"Well," said Elvira, smiling widely. "That is just wonderful. Shall I wait for you to follow me?"

"No, no." Suddenly Donna felt strength course through her. During the past few weeks, her fear of her husband had shrunk substantially, mainly replaced by hatred and rage. She could not allow that fear to ever regain a stronghold again. Nothing could ever be as it was, and sooner or later she would leave him, but until she knew how she was going to do that, she would most certainly proceed with caution. She didn't see any danger in going out tonight though. She knew Marco well enough to know that he wouldn't be back so soon, and the time had come for her to find out more about how real people lived their lives these days.

"Not to worry," she said. "You head off and meet your manure, and I'll be with you in no time."

She waved Elvira off, and hurried inside to get changed. She dug out a pair of ancient skinny jeans that she had only worn once because Marco had smilingly said that they made her look like chubby mutton dressed as silly lamb, pretending to be making a joke, but she knew that he had meant what he said to hurt just as much as it had. His teasing was always injected with venom. She topped them with a gossamer pale blue shirt, and slipped on the silver sandals that to her husband had indicated the taste level of a streetwalker. He'd always insulted the way she used to dress, and made condescending suggestions on the way she should look instead, until she'd just given up and worn mostly stretch pants and t-shirts. He seemed happy with her appearance that way. She grinned at her reflection as she applied mascara to her lashes, vowing to try and find her own sense of style again. It had been too long since she had cared what she looked like.

"Stuff you Marco McGee," she said, grabbed her handbag and skipped out of the house.

Chapter Six

By the time she reached Elvira's smallholding she'd totally run out of steam. Her confidence had evaporated as soon as she'd hit the outskirts of Wilson Springs. She'd taken back roads, but now the thought of being seen by someone who knew Marco brought on a cold lump of fear in her belly. How stupid she was to have thought that she would get away with something like this. The outfit that she'd thought was so cute when she left the house now seemed exactly what Marco had told her it was so long ago. A pathetic attempt by an old woman with the tastes of a tart to look young again, when it was much too late for that. Her brief straying from her usual feeling of being separate from any other human being had been stupid. That knowledge that nobody would ever be on her side, or have her back in times of trouble, came rushing in to replace the tiny belief that she might ever connect with another person, and squashed it right there. She was, as she always would be, totally, completely, absolutely alone. Her home with Marco was all she ever would have. These people didn't know her, and if they ever got to see the mixed up crazy thing that she was inside, they wouldn't want anything to do with her. She, and her life were way too far from normal, but it was what it was. Why risk losing everything for a night out with strangers?

She sat in the idling car for several minutes before shaking herself out of her immobility. She crashed the gears and reversed back towards the gates, then slammed on the brakes and ducked when an air horn blasted from what sounded like the back seat. She glanced over her shoulder to find the way out blocked by a huge rig that clearly had no intention of going in any direction other than forward. The smell of aged manure drifted into her window as she edged out of the truck's way, to be in position to drive out just as soon as the way was clear. She sat hunched over the steering wheel, waiting, suddenly exhausted, and feeling like the biggest loser in the world. She had wasted her life on a demon. She had nothing and nobody, and her trying to grab back any part of it was as useless as it was pitiable. She tried to stop the single tear from squeezing itself from her eye. It was a surprising tear. She hadn't allowed herself to cry for so long that she couldn't remember when last she had.

"Turn your engine off quickly. Best to make a run for the coffee shop before Elmore here squishes you like a bug. I swear he bought his driver's licence in a back alley somewhere, and he has the temper of a poked hornet."

She looked up at Elvira, forgetting the tear now running down her face. The woman stared for a moment, then leaned forward and wiped it away with a grubby thumb.

"Turn it off love, and let's head in for a drink."

Donna didn't argue when Elvira opened her door, and reached in to turn the key in the ignition. She watched impassively as her car's windows were wound up, and it was locked. She turned and led the way through the house to the back, her mind in a turmoil of conflicting certainties that Marco would never find out that she'd done this, and then that he was sure to find out. As she breathed in the damp smell of freshly watered earth, mingled with the scent of thousands of blossoms as she walked slowly through the garden, her spirits lifted slightly, as beauty always made them do, but all the faces turned towards her as she reached the patio of the coffee shop made her want to turn and run.

Elvira nudged her over to an empty wicker chair, before heading into the shop kitchen. She smiled and murmured hellos to the small group sitting around, or lounging on the sofas.

"It's good to see you again."

Donna stared into the weathered face smiling down at her, and tried hard to remember the name that went with it. Not that she could think of anything to say even if she did. A glass appeared in front of her nose.

"What are you having Saul?" Elvira put a large glass canister filled with a rich brown liquid onto the large table, settled into a chair opposite them, winked and raised her own glass before taking a big sip and sighing with pleasure.

"Cheers," she said.

Saul lifted a beer from the floor beside his chair. "Indeed," he said softly, "Cheers."

Donna sipped her drink and gasped. Elvira laughed.

"That's my special chocolate coffee," she said. "My home-made chocolate coffee liqueur potion, one hundred percent guaranteed to put a smile on any dial."

The alcoholic warmth of the the liquid, and the strong scent of cocoa laced coffee was sweet and soothing. She remembered trying very hard to become an alcoholic when she'd had her breakdown, and failing miserably. At the time anything, including daily hangovers, would have felt better than the way she had. She looked up, still not sure what to say. In the tiny time it had taken since she'd arrived, everyone around had moved their chairs closer without her noticing. There was an odd mix of furniture under the large gazebo that led into the small building. Sofas, chairs of all colours and descriptions, occasional tables and dining room tables were scattered around in the most informal way.

Sandy came to sit beside her, closing her laptop and tucking her bare feet up under her the way she'd had them the first time Donna had met her. Elvira introduced her to Margarie and Vincent, both writers like Sandy, and Erika, the recently separated and currently unemployed. It soon became obvious that Elvira, Sandy, Saul and Laurence were the core of the group, and old friends. Sandy's speech was littered with enough profanity to get anyone's attention, but still her sentences were all lyrically magical. Donna liked her immediately.

"I can't imagine writing a book," she said, slightly star struck. "How do you think up new things to write about?"

"I don't," said Sandy. "They just arrive. It's funny though. I think that there's this nebulous place, all around us, and in our minds and souls, filled with the amorphous foetuses of every story ever told, and every story to be told. When one of these babies just take root and begin to grow, well then, you just have to write what you see. You can't ever force it. I always think that as I write, that somewhere out there, in some other reality, the words I write are spoken out loud. I never plan, and I never know where I'll be taken."

Donna remembered Laurence from before. His brooding good looks gave her the chills. She knew better now than to trust anyone with such a perfect facade. He could be rotten to the core, so she avoided directing any conversation his way. They all chatted idly about the week they'd had, and when she commented that it was interesting that so many of them were writers, they laughed.

"Everyone's a writer these days darling," said Sandy.

"Sort of true," said Vincent, with a slightly pained expression, "but not everyone's good at it."

"We all love Elvira's little garden here," said Saul. "There isn't anywhere other than Charly's to get together around town, so most of us earn our crusts lurking around here with friends."

"And it's so much nicer than hanging around all alone at home banging away at the laptop. The lunches are out of this world too. This is a good place to work," said Laurence, smiling at their hostess. "Any place Elvira is, is a good place to be."

Donna's hackles rose. Smooth. He reminded her too much of Marco when he was in spadework mode. She couldn't suppress a sudden grin. Experts on the narcissistic psychotic called the episodes when they sucked up to their victims hoovering. Trust Marco to come up with his own name for something he probably never knew existed outside of his own sick thought patterns. She leaned forward to pick up her newly delivered glass of wine, and looked up to see Laurence staring right at her. She recoiled.

"You look so familiar," he said, still smiling. "I'm sure we've met before."

She shook her head, barely able to stop herself from a rude retort, and turned to Erika, who had not said much since they'd been there, apart from the fact that finding a job seemed to be impossible.

"What sort work are you hoping to find?" she asked.

Erika looked at her with tired eyes, twirling the stem of her glass but so far not having touched the wine in it.

"Anything," she said. "I don't know really. I haven't worked for so long, I don't know what, if anything, I'm capable of anymore. But if I don't find something soon, I'm going to be in trouble."

"You'll find something love," said Elvira. "And until you do, you know that you have us."

"That's right," said Laurence. "You know we'll help in any way we can."

"What about you?" asked Erika. "What do you do?"

Donna quailed under their combined gaze. What did she do? What had she ever done? She had a degree in horticulture, but she'd only worked for a few years. She'd married Marco, quickly had Shelley, and before she realised what it would mean, they'd moved here, because the property had been dirt cheap and close enough to where Marco worked. Then her sole job had been caring for the two of them. In those days, money had been scarce. All of her savings had gone into Marco's first fledgling business, and she'd soon realised as he'd jumped from one enterprise to another before finally settling into the one he had now, which did seem to make money, that she would never get to spend a cent that she hadn't earned herself. The times she had mentioned that she'd like to get back to work after Marco had insisted that Shelley go to boarding school, he'd reacted so badly that she eventually stopped mentioning it. She'd never forgiven him for insisting on boarding school, just because he had gone to one, and said it was the only way to educate a child properly. She'd rattled around mourning the loss of her daughter, and blaming herself for it, while believing that there was nothing she could do about it. What could she say to these people now?

"Donna has the most impressive private gardens I've ever seen," said Elvira. "She has plants that I doubt grow in many other places in the country. Absolutely beautiful."

Donna smiled at her, grateful for the save, but ashamed that she didn't have a proper job to talk about, or any reason to exist if she thought about it. Her gardening was her hobby, that was all, something that she'd done to try and stay sane, and having an interesting collection of plants wasn't going to put food on her table.

No one else saw it like that though. More than their writing and their other work, these people were clearly lovers of the soil first and foremost. Immediately they were all questioning her. Surprised at their genuine interest, she found herself telling them about some of the things she'd done over the years, the hybrids she'd created, and the collection of rare and strange species she'd accumulated. They were really keen to see all the old equipment that had been in the farmhouse when the McGees had moved in. Donna had refurbished some of the old things, and now used them to make her own essential oils, because buying her favourite perfumes was no longer an option.

As the sun went down, and the wine flowed, Donna relaxed completely, laughing at silly jokes, and feeling free for the first time in decades to just be herself. This, the camaraderie, and the firming of new friendships made her much bolder than she could ever have imagined, and when they all asked to see her gardens, she said yes without any hesitation. When it was time to leave, Elvira promised to call the next day as she gathered the glasses onto a tray, and Laurence walked with her through the dimly lit parking area to her car.

"Would you like to go for a coffee before you go home?" he asked, reaching for her hand.

Donna blushed, appalled. Of course he was another like Marco, trying to hit on a married woman. He probably had a wife and children waiting for him at home, and a couple of girlfriends scattered around town for good measure.

"So, do you always ask other men's wives out for coffee?" she asked.

His jaw clenched, and he looked down at the hand that she'd forgotten still rested in his. She followed his gaze. Of course. No wedding ring. She'd lost it and her engagement ring three years into her marriage. Marco had twisted that nicely, insisting that she wouldn't have lost them if she'd loved him. Why didn't she wear them all the time anyway? He'd refused to replace them, and she'd just made excuses over the years when anyone did wonder why she wore no rings.

Laurence dropped her hand like a hot coal. "I'm sorry," he said. "And no. I don't ask other men's wives out. Ever."

Wishing that the earth would swallow her, she muttered her own apologies without being able to look him in the eye, and got into her car and out of the gate as fast as she could.

Chapter Seven

Donna opened an eye. She was on the couch again, and the hammers in her head belatedly warned her of the dangers of mixing strong liqueur with too many glasses of wine. She looked at her watch. Five o'clock. If Marco had come home he'd still be asleep. She tiptoed upstairs to find the bed untouched, and breathed a large sigh of relief.

It was only after she'd had a bath, and was pulling an old pair of jeans on that she remembered inviting them all to see her gardens. As she lost her balance and fell backwards onto her bed, the memory of the final words in the parking area with Laurence came back. Groaning, she pulled herself up and finished dressing, wild thoughts rushing through her mind. She had to undo what she had done, and very, very quickly too.

She took her coffee out into the crisp morning air, and sat on one of the stained wooden benches in her rose garden, planning her day. First, she'd phone Elvira, and make sure that their fledgling friendship ended straight away, and that nobody other than herself ever set foot in her secret place ever again. And Laurence—. Guilt and embarrassment vied for prime position. But there was nothing she could do about Laurence. She forced the look of shock and shame that she'd seen on his face before leaping into her car out of her mind. She'd never seen a look like that on Marco's face, no matter what he'd done. And he'd done some pretty awful things.

With all of the trouble she'd been getting herself into the past few days, she hadn't given Marco much thought. Now she allowed herself to wonder where he was. Probably with Jackie or one of the other string of women he generally had waiting in the wings for him. She wasn't at all jealous of him having sex with other women. The thought of Marco touching her in any way had been repulsive to her for years, and she was grateful that he never tried to anymore. But the feeling of being worth so little that she could be left alone like this, without so much as a text message, by the man who expected her utmost attention and respect at all times, brought on her usual anxiety now.

Nothing compared to the feeling of being totally alone in the world. And she was alone. Nobody would ever catch her if she fell. Nobody would ever stand up for her. Nobody would ever again touch or caress her. Love her. She remembered an incident, a few years after her marriage. They'd been at a club. When Marco drank he took the greatest pleasure in insulting as many people as he could. Their looks, or race, culture or religion. All of these things were his favourite subjects for painful jibes. She couldn't remember the amount of times he'd been punched. On this occasion she'd been in the ladies room, only to return to raised voices and a large man leaning over with Marco's shirt clutched in a giant fist. Marco had been laughing.

She'd joined the group, terrified as she had been, and stood beside her husband. One of the women in the group had asked her what she wanted, and when she'd told her who she was, the woman had thrown her drink in her face. The large man had let go of Marco and apologised for his girlfriend's behaviour. Marco had stood back and smiled smugly down at her, enjoying her humiliation. The group had left, Marco ordered another drink, and she had gone to sit and wait for him in the car, with the cold, stinking alcohol trickling through her hair and down her blouse. No apology. No asking if she was alright. No caring at all. There had been many times like that, and now Donna knew exactly what being alone really meant.

She sighed, and pulled her phone out of her pocket. Best get the call over with. Elvira accepted her statement that she was going to stay with her daughter for a few months and wouldn't be around. She asked about Donna's garden and also accepted Donna's assurance that there were automated sprinklers in place and no help would be needed. She sounded distracted and not her usual laughing self, and Donna ended the connection feeling very fretful. Even though she'd got what she wanted, not ever having to interact with Elvira and her friends again, the thought that Elvira had realised what a stupid waste of space she was, and was more than likely glad to end contact with her, was deeply saddening.

Chapter Eight

Marco stayed away for two full weeks, and for the very first time she didn't care at all. These two weeks had been a revelation to Donna. When her phone remained silent, and no cars had pulled into the drive, she occasionally found small pockets of time when her body completely relaxed for the first time since she'd met her husband. She marvelled at the strangeness of the feeling. No tense muscles. No feeling of constantly waiting for something awful to happen. She was accustomed to being nervous all the time, and the absence of those feelings made her realise that living without her husband could mean that she need never feel them again.

She worked in her gardens, slept sprawled out across the bed, waking more refreshed and invigorated every day. She explored the new world on her computer, took long indulgent bubble baths, and read obsessively. She had been shocked at how many books there were about narcissistic psychopaths, and even more astonished at the similarity of all of the stories to her own life. These creatures were more common than anyone could imagine, and easily recognisable if you knew the signs. She giggled a little at Marco then. Such a very common profile, and him believing that he was so incredible, so wonderful and unique, when all he really was, was sick in the head and common as muck. The giggles didn't last very long. Maybe his deviation was more common that she would have thought, but that didn't make him any less dangerous.

No normally functioning human being would ever imagine that such signs existed. That such people existed. If she hadn't lived it herself, she wouldn't have believed it any more than she believed that reptilian aliens walked the Earth. Shaking her head, she laughed loudly at the thought that maybe that was true too. Maybe these psychos were all actually lizards in disguise. Eventually, sick to her stomach from all the memories brought back by reading the stories of others, Donna closed the final book, and decided that she needed to heal herself. She didn't know how she would do this, or how she would fill that empty, aching void within herself that had formed over the years. It occurred to her that the tightly shut, inward looking person she had become now was just as inhuman as Marco was, only dead inside rather than unable to see outward because of total and absolute self love. Donna was hiding somewhere deep inside, and with each memory she was being forced back out, tiny pieces at a time. That little true remnant of herself that remained didn't want to come out, and see the truth. That little Donna remnant was still too afraid.

The tension returned the minute she heard his car pull into the drive. Racing to hide her laptop, she tried to guess what, if any, excuse she would be given for this extended absence. He was sitting on the couch when she got downstairs with the remote in his hand, and his eyes on the television. He looked up and smiled briefly. She stood looking down at him, until it sunk in that he wasn't going to say anything. This was going to be one of those pretend nothing happened times. She went to the kitchen and started washing vegetables for supper. The familiar painful knots had quickly returned to the muscles at the base of her neck and down her shoulder blades.

She slapped a cabbage down on the chopping board, and chopped it with more aggression than precision, furious at the effect Marco had on her merely by being in the same space. She wasn't a coward. She knew that if he ever had physically attacked her, she would have returned the favour with bonuses, and she'd always had the suspicion that the fact that he realised that too was the only reason he hadn't.

There had been an intruder on the grounds once. A drug addicted hobo, so far away from reality that he had stood at the open window of Marco's study and just started jabbering unintelligibly. Marco had screamed like a girl and ducked under his desk, not at all concerned that she had been sitting on the chair directly under the window, taking notes for a presentation he was due to give.

She slammed the knife down on the counter. A coward had put her in the state that she was in. Their marriage had ended shortly after it had begun, and yet here she still was. Afraid of what? She leaned forward, holding on to the sink, eyes tightly closed, trying to remember what her normal had been. When had she forsaken herself and given over her life to another? How had she got to this place?

Her mind tried its usual trick of shutting down, but this time she wouldn't let it. The only way that she had been able to drag herself upwards after her breakdown had been to shut herself off from intense feelings. She'd blocked the memories of the many years before, and enforced a modicum of civility in her marriage. She couldn't take the weekly screaming, draining, infinitely destructive fights any more. Marco had backed down for once, when he must have seen that she was serious. That had been the final time that she had rushed, crying, out of the house into the darkness outside. She'd walked down the road for a while, and then firmly decided that she would never spend a night outside again. Nights trying to think of a way, any way, to get away from him, before giving up and crawling back in the morning, freezing cold and in a state of shock. There had been too many nights like that. And he had never once come after her, because he honestly didn't care if she came to any harm. And because he knew that she'd be back. He knew she had nowhere to go because he had made it so. She'd always find him tucked up in bed, sleeping the sleep of the totally uncaring, before bouncing happily out of bed and carrying on as if nothing had happened.

So the insane vicious fighting had stopped. But there never was any closure. No reason she could ever find for the way he behaved, and she could see no way out, so she gave up, always hoping that he would change one day, and see how badly he was hurting her. She silently accepted his arrogance, condescension and rudeness, trying not to see the pleasure he derived from her hard to conceal reactions. She told herself that if she expected nothing from him, it would hurt less when she got nothing from him. She knew now that that is exactly what he wanted. He enjoyed having a beautiful home, cared for by a beautiful wife. A wife who allowed him to do exactly what he pleased. He also enjoyed telling people about how absolutely insane she was. Jealous and insane, and he loved coming across as a good man who stayed with a woman who apparently treated him really badly in every way.

He'd played her like a puppet all these years with his insidious sniping, purposefully trying to anger her, and belittling her. His ridiculous denials, and lies that made no sense at all. Even now that she was sure that she would never feel completely safe, or trust anyone again, she still went along with his lies. She said nothing when they came her way, and she supported and covered up for him when he lied to others, even though she knew that those in his circles, his circles consisting only of those who worked for him, thought that she was a sour, stupid, frigid woman. She'd overheard him telling them so more than once. They felt sorry for him. And after all that, still she had supported him. She'd still felt pity for him when she thought he might be hurt, no matter how badly he hurt her. And she'd still felt the need to protect him when she had thought him vulnerable.

She opened her eyes, a little afraid of the combined shame and rage that was making her tremble. Again that desire to just run out of the door, and keep on running without ever looking back nearly got the better of her. She took a deep breath and tried to push that urge away. She couldn't run out of the door. She had nowhere to go. No one to run to. No money, and no talent to earn enough to keep herself alive. Marco had made sure of that.

As she prepared the rest of the meal, she kept asking herself what the worst thing that could happen to her could be. What thing would she most regret on her death bed. And every time the only answer she could give was staying where she was.

Marco took his plate of food to his study and closed the door. Donna took a bottle of wine and a glass onto the patio, and dove deep within herself again. If she could just remember everything. If she could look back know and see it all, with her new knowledge of what he really was, maybe she could find a way out of her private little hell.

Chapter Nine

Donna laid out Marco's breakfast, then sat sipping her coffee watching him eat, hating every movement his mouth made as he chewed. She jumped when her phone rang, lips tightening as she watched his arm snake out and pick it up before she could. He snorted and tossed it into her outstretched hand.

"*Happy birthday Mom.*"

"Thank you love."

Donna tried to sound cheerful for Shelley's sake, but she hated her birthdays. She loved the presents her daughter had either made or bought for her over the years, but she hated the feeling of not being loved or liked enough by anyone else to even get so much as a card.

"Thank you for what?" interrupted Marco.

"I've deposited some cash into your account Mom," said Shelley. "I know that's not a proper present, but I just haven't got the time to come out there now. I've made you a pendant though. I'll bring it next time I see you."

"There really was no need—," said Donna as her husband snatched the phone from her ear.

"Thank you for what?" he repeated.

Donna watched as he listened, blinked, and disconnected the call. She cringed, but knew that her daughter would understand. She'd phone her back when Marco left the house.

"Happy birthday," he said, wiping his mouth and pulling out his wallet.

"Here's the grocery money. I haven't had time to transfer it, so cash for now," he said, dropping a small wad of notes in front of her. "Things are a little tight this month. I need a jar of eye cream. Today if possible."

She counted it after he'd gone. Not a cent more than usual. And get the eye cream today if possible meant to definitely get it today. She'd have to cut back on something else this week.

"Happy birthday Donna," she murmured, getting up to wash the dishes.

*

She thought that her heart would jump right out of her chest when the hand clamped down on her arm as she stood in line at the pharmacy.

"You're back early," said Elvira, smiling. "Why didn't you call?"

Donna stammered. She'd completely forgotten that the possibility of bumping into someone from the coffee shop in Wilson Springs was quite high.

"We'll pop over the road to Charly's, grab a bite to eat, and have a catch up," said Elvira, giving her a little nudge. "I'm starving."

All the strength drained out of Donna. She didn't have the energy right now to try and pretend, or to try and make excuses to keep people out of her life.

Elvira was her usual bubbly self, chatting away as she tucked into her large slice of pie.

"So. How did your visit go?" she asked. "Are you back to stay now?"

Donna stared down at her plate for a while, and then said, "I didn't go anywhere."

Elvira nodded. Seemingly unsurprised, she carried on chewing.

"I lied," said Donna.

"I know," said Elvira.

"How did you know?" The shame from admitting to her lie gave way to blossoming terror. Had she been spying on her?

Elvira put her fork down and sipped her coffee.

"I always know when someone lies," she said. "I generally don't like to look any further or invade anyone's privacy, but you—. I am psychic you know."

Elvira dug in her bag and put another of her business cards on the table between them, tapping her finger beneath the word 'psychic'. Donna laughed, hot coffee burning back up her throat and into her nose.

"I don't believe in that sort of thing," she said.

Elvira leaned back in her chair and smiled.

"You're frightened," she said softly. "Terrified. You feel powerless, trapped, and alone. More alone than anyone I've ever met. There is a dark force in your life. A force that wishes you nothing but harm. Your fear is valid. But you don't want anyone to know about what's been done. You're wrongly ashamed, and you don't believe that anyone can help you."

Donna felt her cheeks grow icy cold as the blood drained from her face. She carefully placed her cup on the table and fished in her pocket for a tissue. Tears welled up for the first time in decades, and she knew that she wasn't going to hold them in this time. They came as she ran for her car, people staring at her as she fumbled with her keys, unable to stop the visceral sobs wracking her frame.

Finally safe in the warm cocoon, she dropped her face into her hands and let the tears fall. It hadn't been so much the words that the woman had said, but the sympathy and care in the voice. She could never have imagined that anyone would know how she felt, and she didn't understand why Elvira or anyone else would suddenly give a damn. She heard the passenger door open, and felt the car rock a little as someone got in. A warm hand squeezed her shoulder, and made her cry harder. Finally the heaving, tearing sobs subsided, and she breathed easier. She was too embarrassed to take her hands from her face.

"Funny thing," said Elvira. "Sometimes when a soul can take no more, they put themselves just where they should be. I don't believe that everything is coincidental. You don't have to be alone. You have people who already consider you friend. People willing to help you escape from your darkness."

Donna sniffed, and roughly wiped her face. She didn't believe that anyone could help her. Why would strangers even consider any involvement in the mess that was her life? Even though those words had hit the nail on the head, she was sure that they had been a lucky guess. If Elvira really knew what was happening, she would run for the hills. Nobody would be prepared to help her do what she needed to do, and she would never dream of asking for help in the form of money or accommodation from her own daughter, let alone a stranger. Her swollen eyes hurt, but even though she was embarrassed by her outburst, it felt as though some dark abscess had burst within her soul and poured out of her. Washed out in the liquid of her tears. She felt lighter.

"Do you want to talk about it?" asked Elvira.

"I—. I can't. I don't think I can." She slowly turned to face the woman in the passenger seat.

Elvira took her hand and patted it, smiling. "Yes," she said. "I see. And you can't possibly come to the coffee shop today because you're washing your hair or have an urgent pile of turnips to peel?"

Donna hiccupped and laughed. "I must look horrible," she said.

"No," said Elvira, handing over a pile of napkins that she'd lifted from the table at Charly's when she'd run out. "No. You don't must look horrible at all. How about I follow you home and we can chat in peace?"

Donna laughed some more. She pulled down the mirror and wiped the running mascara from beneath her eyes. She was very wary of sharing any part of her life with any normal person. What if it really was all in her mind? All her fault, just as Marco always said. Then she shook her head. No. It wasn't her. She had to finally realise that. It was not her. It was, and always had been him.

"Yes," she said. "That will be good. Thank you."

"Hah!" said Elvira. "Thank you! You're harder to make friends with than a sack full of mules. On your way then. I'll be right behind you."

Donna drove slowly, waiting for the landscaper's van to catch up. The thought of having someone to talk to, someone who genuinely cared, was joyous and horrifying beyond words.

Chapter Ten

"You think he has what?"

Elvira's slight frown brought fluttering moths of fear to her belly. Maybe she *was* wrong. Maybe she was trying to justify her own shortcomings by blaming someone else.

"Malignant narcissistic personality disorder," she mumbled.

Elvira looked puzzled. "Never heard of it. But fair enough," she said. "He's most definitely an evil asshole. Call it what you like." She leaned forward and topped both of their glasses up with the chilled light wine they had opted for rather than more coffee. "Sandy's a psychiatrist you know? She'd probably know about that. Although she didn't practice very long before she married her own evil asshole. Now that she's finally got rid of him, she writes."

Donna relaxed, smiling at hearing Marco being called an asshole by another. She had called him far worse in her mind over the years. She hadn't even begun to tell her whole story, still too embarrassed, but she'd shared a lot, and Elvira had not once registered any sort of disbelief, and she never asked her why she had stayed. She heartily recommended that Donna leave though. And as fast as she possibly could. Elvira put her glass down and tapped her watch.

"I must get back," she said. "You're welcome to arrive at Roses anytime, day or night if you need to, and you'll be welcome to stay as long as you like. Phone me if you have any problem. Really. I mean it. You don't have to stay here. You'll be surprised how much you'll find you can do. I see that for now you honestly believe that you can't leave, but remember you're not alone anymore. You really must join us more often. Nobody is meant to be an island, and certainly nobody should be forced to be one." She raised an enquiring brow. "Will you promise me to ask for help when you need it?"

Donna nodded, exhausted after her outburst, but a new strength was growing in her, and slowly but surely she was seeing glimpses of reality. Her current reality, and the reality that she needed. She needed to start being human again, and that meant being with other humans. Real ones, not psychotic pretenders like Marco.

"Thank you," she said. "Thank you for being so nice to me."

Marco pulled into the drive just as Donna opened the door. She stopped in her tracks, blocking the doorway, hand frozen on the doorknob, and completely at a loss at what to do. Elvira stood silently behind her, watching him inspect her van, frown, and walk briskly to the house. He stopped, looking down at his wife, the chill in his gaze freezing her further to the spot.

"Problem?" he asked.

Donna shook her head and moved aside. He looked from one woman to the other, taking in the long streaks of Prussian blue in Elvira's hair, her worn, tight jeans, and the flowing retro hippy blouse above them. For a few seconds his tightly pursed lips and ice cold eyes gave the impression that he was about to lose his temper, but then he smiled down at her. With a sinking heart, Donna realised that he'd decided on honey rather than acid to get rid of this one, even though Elvira was most certainly not the sort of person he'd ever be seen in public with, she was still a beautiful woman. He turned to look at her, smiling.

"Who's this then?"

"Elvira," said Elvira, seeing Donna's ashen face. She stepped forward with her hand held out. Marco looked down at it as if it were priceless treasure, and took it gently in both of his own.

And so her tentative hope that she'd met a true friend withered and died, just the way her hopes always did. This would be the end. She'd never come across a single woman who Marco had failed to charm when he set his mind to it. She would have preferred it this time if he had chosen his more often used condescending discourtesy when he came to meet someone who he thought might be a threat to his control of her. There would be no coffee shops and new friendships now.

"It's a pleasure to meet you Elvira," he said, his tone sensual as melted chocolate. He let go of her hand, and turned to Donna. "I never knew we were expecting company today. You never mentioned you were having a friend over."

She shook her head, speechless, and finally looked at Elvira, ready for that floppy smile. That dazed expression she always saw, of a woman who thought that she had just found her love at first sight soul mate. Marco's little hand embraces always had that effect. There was nothing floppy about the smile she saw though. Elvira was smiling charmingly, but her eyes were steely.

"My visit was unannounced Mr McGee," she said, in that unmistakable tone of those educated and rich enough to be very comfortable in their own skin.

Donna blinked. Even the way Elvira stood seemed different now, oozing power and confidence. If this had been the woman she'd met when she went looking for tomatoes, she doubted that she would have said more than two words. Nothing irritated her more than the uber-wealthy country club wives.

"I am the trustee for the Gardens for Grandparents Charity," drawled Elvira. "My father started it a few years ago. You may know him from your business dealings. Gabriel Jordan Young." She grinned at him, seemingly oblivious to his widened eyes, and sudden intake of breath.

"We've been hearing such good things about your wife's gardening abilities, and seeing as how we didn't have her number, and didn't want to disturb you at your place of business, I was despatched to try and rope her in to join our team."

Marco pushed his hands in his pockets, all sensuality replaced with the most beguiling smile in the world. He nodded briskly.

"Of course," he said. "We both love our gardening. I really wish I'd been here when you arrived." He glanced over at Donna, standing slack-jawed in her cluelessness. "You should have phoned me my love. Never mind though, I'm here now. Would you care to join us for a few minutes more Elvira? I'd love to hear more about your Gardens for Grandparents."

Elvira allowed herself to be ushered to the patio, and smiled smugly at Marco's departing back as he rushed off to fetch wine and glasses. Donna trailed in, not knowing what was happening, and could only shake her head in confusion. Elvira leaned forward and patted her hand.

"Just go with the flow," she whispered and winked. "Trust me."

Donna accepted a glass of wine from her husband and sat back in her chair.

"It's always wonderful to meet couples who garden together," said Elvira. "It's really *such* a pity that neither of you have the time to spare to join our programme."

Marco coughed so hard that a little wine shot from his mouth.

Elvira stood up and strolled over to the trellis separating the tiled floor from the immaculate lawn. She bent down and plucked a pale bloom. "Such beautiful flowers you have here." She frowned, and peered more closely at it. "Although I don't recognise this particular specimen." She turned to look at Marco, holding the delicate flower out to him.

"What species would this be Mr McGee?"

Donna got such a shock when Elvira had plucked that flower, that she didn't notice Marco's desperate look in her direction, nor his pretence of continuing his fit of coughing. She jumped out of her chair, and snatched the flower from the outstretched hand, crushing it in her palm.

"Campion Selene Tomentosa," she muttered, before sitting down, and downing the wine remaining in her glass.

"Yes," said Marco, over his fit of spluttering remarkably quickly. "Planted that one myself last year." He smiled at Donna. "Now, about this wonderful charitable cause Elvira needs help for. What's this I hear about lack of time? Of course you *must* help." His lips tightened. "You have all the time in the world, and it would be extremely unfeeling of us not to want to give our usually wasted time to the elderly and alone."

Donna had never heard of Gardens for Grandparents in her life, had no idea what she was expected to say, and was reeling from both Marco's apparent desperate desire to give Elvira whatever she wanted, as well as from the careless plucking of one of the rarest flowers on the planet. A flower that she shouldn't rightly own. She looked at Elvira for help, and found her bent over the plant again, inspecting it carefully. Finally she stood up, and looked knowingly at Donna.

"I wouldn't like you to feel in any way obligated Mrs McGee, but most of the ladies donate at least eight hours a week of their time. Most of us donate much, much more though. I myself host a wine and cheese evening once a week for the old ladies, while the gentlemen are treated to a lovely session of night bowls. It would be wonderful if you could join us ladies, and it would be an absolute blessing if Mr McGee would like to join the gentlemen for bowls.

Marco paled. Donna wanted to laugh out loud at what the thought of spending a minute of his time with a group of elderly bowls playing men must be doing to him.

He smiled a slightly tighter smile at Elvira. "Unfortunately there's too much happening at work for me right now. But soon. Definitely soon. Donna on the other hand, would be happy to put in just as many hours as you do, I'm sure." He turned a flinty gaze on his wife. "Wouldn't you?"

"We'll work something out," said Elvira, in a bright and friendly tone at odds with the anger in her eyes. She put her glass down and started towards the door. "For now I have to be going. I'll phone you Mrs McGee, if you'd let me have your number, and we can arrange to get started."

Donna merely nodded, went through the pretence of swopping numbers for the first time, and silently followed a very chatty Marco as he escorted Elvira to her van.

"I have yet to have the pleasure of meeting your Father," he said. "It's been such a busy few years."

"Oh," said Elvira, "I'm sure you'll meet him soon. We're very close, the two of us, and I like to make sure that we spend time together often."

They watched the van pull out into the road before Marco turned abruptly.

"Are you trying to bloody ruin me woman?"

Donna shook her head in disgust and walked away. She was not prepared to listen to more of his ranting right now. She opened another bottle of wine and headed back out to the patio, with him hot on her heels.

"Do you know who Gabriel Gordon Young *is?*"

She topped up her own glass only, and banged the bottle down on the table.

"No," she said. "I don't."

"Only one of the richest men in the country. He owns most of Wilson Springs. And it's well known that anyone he favours will get unimaginable deals. If he likes someone he gives them things. Money. Sounds like he's soft in the head, but I don't give a crap about that. I need to meet him, and for once in your life you can do a couple of days work instead of swanning around here like the lady of the manor, spending my money and sitting on your backside. You owe me."

Once again she'd been wrong in thinking that she was finished being hurt by Marco, so the sharp pain that accompanied his words made her want to cry for the second time today. Twice in one day. Twice in a decade. She took a deep breath. This would not be a good time to take the bait and lash out in hurt and anger.

"What is it that you want me to do?"

He sneered at her. She recognised the expression of disgust at her apparent weakness combined with the glint of pleasure in his eye at his easy victory. She'd seen it so many times after she'd just got too tired to argue.

"You like to pretend that you're some fancy gardener. Well now's your chance. You put in maximum hours digging in a couple of old bastard's gardens. And you attend every one of that woman's stupid granny parties. Do whatever she asks you to do. Pretend to be her friend." He sneered. "You wouldn't know what that felt like, would you? Having friends. Just pretend. Until I'm in with her father. Then you can go back to whatever shit you get up to on your long lazy days."

Donna had leaned over and put her face in her hands as soon as she realised what he was saying. She wanted to laugh. Run around the house and laugh as loud as she could. He thought that he was making her do something that she didn't want to do. She'd become so reclusive these last years that she must have given him the impression that she actively hated company. Having to do something that she would hate, and that would make her more miserable than she already was, would just be icing on the cake for Marco. But already she could feel the tiny breath of freedom. A small loosening of the vicelike grip of black darkness that had held her soul for so long. When she looked up at him she knew that all he would see on her face would be anger. The anger that she had willed to replace the joy that bubbled within her now. Angry faces were easy to fake when you knew anger so very well. The grin on his face was strangely accompanied in her mind by the chittering sound of a demon. The more she looked at him these days, the less human he became in her eyes, and she knew that the times of accepting her life with him were over.

Chapter Eleven

Elvira arrived early with more seedlings, and they quickly loaded up barrows to take down to the old farmstead.

"I still find it so strange that you've kept such a large secret for so long," she said, keeping pace with a tense, silent, almost sprinting Donna, who didn't trust Marco not to show up after his totally unexpected arrival yesterday. "I'm looking forward to finding out about more of your secrets too. Like where you laid your hands on that Campion for instance. That's as rare as unicorn crap, and I'm pretty sure it's only to be seen in two or three other places on the planet. You could probably be arrested just for having it. I really must have one of my own now."

Donna placed the last tray of plants on the ground and dusted her hands off before they headed briskly back up to the terraces.

"Secrets," she said, smiling. "I still have no idea what happened with you and Marco yesterday. Nor do I have any clue about this charity of yours. Is it real?"

"It's real alright, although I might have withheld a tiny bit of information from your husband. He really walked right into that."

"And your father? Marco wants to meet him more than anything."

Elvira chuckled. "I bet he does. My father doesn't go out any more. Doesn't leave his mansion. Doesn't leave his room to be quite honest. Still. No reason not to use him as a carrot."

"Shame," said Donna. "Is he not well?"

"You could say that. It's all in his head though. I'm not sure what happened to him, but around two years ago, he suddenly started splashing money around, right after my mother died. Although it couldn't have been that. She was a tyrant, and it must have been a blessed relief to see her go."

"Your mother—."

Donna couldn't conceal her shock at the thought of anyone talking so callously of a dead parent. She still felt love for her own mother, even though she hadn't been a very good one. Her entire childhood had been about shame and fear. Her mother had worked long hours for very little income, and from her earliest memory, Donna had been a key child. Always getting lost, and severely beaten for doing so when her mother had had to collect her from the shopkeepers or policemen who had called the number she always carried with her. Wandering in places no child should be.

Growing up, it had only ever been her and her mother. Occasionally there would be visits from aunts and cousins, but those had always been tense and hurried. She'd gotten close to her cousins when she'd moved into her own place, but they'd disappeared from her life when Marco had moved in.

She didn't know who her father was, or whether he still lived or was dead. She often dreamed of him arriving one day to rescue her. Her mother had moved from one lover to the next, and there had never been any money for proper food. Donna was brought up mostly on bread and sweet tea, and sometimes nothing at all. Her clothes were second hand, and so were her school uniforms. Her mother had never once attended a school event or meeting. Never paid her school fees on time. They'd moved from one run down flat to the next, and she'd never stayed in one place for long enough to make friends. She'd worked hard to put herself through college, and finally was independent and working an extremely well paying job, with new friends for the first time in her life, and a normal future ahead of her before she'd met Marco. But still she loved her mother. She understood how hard it must have been for her to survive, and she forgave her the neglect and the hardships.

Elvira scowled.

"My mother was never a mother to me. I was brought up by nannies," she said. "All she cared about was money and looking good. And she treated my father like crap right up until she was killed. Killed in a botched robbery attempt. I wouldn't blame my dad if he had orchestrated that, and I've often wondered. He turned into a strange shadow of his former self after that. Frightened of his own shadow. Giving huge amounts of cash away after a lifetime of being as tight as a shark's arse. In fact it was the first time in my life that he'd given much more than fifty or a hundred bucks to me. But by then I didn't need his money. I bought Roses with money I earned myself. Gardens for Grandparents was my idea though. I figured that if he was going to throw his millions into the wind, some of it may as well be put to good use. He was delighted to help. Seems to me that half the country send their elderly to be forgotten and die in Wilson Springs. Do you know how many retirement homes there are around here?"

Donna shook her head, heading into her kitchen and filling the kettle. Elvira settled herself into a chair.

"Eight," she said. "In and around town there are eight. And most of them are the most depressing places you will ever see. Tiny little flatlets with tiny little patches of garden, and filled with the loneliest people in the world. Old, often sick or in pain, discarded and forgotten."

Donna felt a huge pang of guilt imagining these poor old people, considering the amount of time she spent feeling sorry for herself. She had a huge house and the most fantastical garden in the world, and yet she too had felt like the loneliest soul on the planet. She put the coffee on the table and sat down.

"Yes," she said. "I was wondering what it is that you wanted me to do."

"You don't have to do anything that you don't want to do love." Elvira dunked a biscuit into her coffee. "It just came to me at the time that your husband would do quite a lot to get what he wants, and that is fairly obviously a chunk of my old man's money. It seemed like the perfect solution to getting you out of this beautiful prison more often. You have to start living your own life. Living as *you*. Soon you'll see that there's nothing in the world truly preventing you from walking out of this house, away from the awful man who has you feeling so trapped, forever. Our little Roses club all spend a couple of hours a week working on the gardens of the home's residents. You can come along with me now if you like. I'm off to see a lovely little lady called Lou, long time resident of Rainbow Acres. Laurence usually does Miss Lou, but he's training a bunch of his computer geeks tomorrow."

Donna nodded enthusiastically. The thought of getting out of the house without having to make up an excuse, and interacting with real, normal people made her more excited than she could remember feeling.

"I'd really love that." She couldn't stop the broad grin from spreading and turning into a chuckle of glee.

*

Lou was a very little lady indeed. Donna and Elvira each sat in one of two tiny armchairs in her small flat, while she bustled around setting up a beautiful antique tea set with a small plate of homemade peanut butter biscuits.

"So," she said handing them each a porcelain cup. "It's wonderful to meet you."

Donna looked into the bluest eyes she'd ever seen, twinkling at her from the wrinkled old face.

"Likewise," she said, uncomfortable and self-conscious now that she was here, having been stopped and chatted to by several of the residents on their way from the car park to Lou's place.

"I'm so grateful to all of you." Lou sank slowly backwards into her chair, gripping tightly onto the arms. The action was clearly painful, certainly painful to watch without jumping up to help. Donna almost had before she saw the almost imperceptible shaking of Elvira's head.

"How's the pain Miss Lou?" Elvira asked.

The bright blue eyes skittered anxiously between the two of them before she answered.

"Not too bad today," she said. "Saul brought me my—."

Elvira shot out of her chair, coughing loudly, droplets of tea flying through the air.

"Dearie me," said Lou, blushing. "Must have gone down the wrong pipe."

Elvira pulled a tissue from her pocket and wiped her reddened face.

Donna sat back and watched this odd display without saying anything. She knew a fake cough meant to stop someone saying something when she heard it though. Marco did it all the time. What on Earth could Saul have brought the old lady that Elvira didn't want her to know about? Lou talked about her arthritis, the procedure she was putting off having on her hip, and her firm belief that her children would be bringing her grandchildren to see her soon, even though they hadn't since they'd arranged for her to come here over a year ago. Then she led them to her tiny patch of garden through a glass door.

Donna's eyes widened as she looked left and right. There were no fences or partitions between the resident's gardens, but the boundaries were made perfectly clear by the differences in each one. Each small vibrantly coloured garden exuded bounteous health. She blinked and then brought her focus to the one she was in. Elvira hunkered down to deadhead a small bed of multi-coloured miniature rosebushes with Lou leaning on her cane behind her, chatting away.

Donna walked slowly around, admiring the talent that had managed to pack so much into such a small space. Cherry tomatoes tumbled gaily from stakes set into a bed of marigolds. Cleverly planted in amongst the flowers in the narrow beds that flanked the patch of lawn grew sorrel, lettuce, brinjals and other edible plants. A lot of thought had gone into making this a functional as well as beautiful place, with food growing in amongst the flowers. She looked back at Elvira who was still busily wielding her secateurs, and then started pulling the few weeds that had begun to sprout here and there.

It was tucked neatly underneath and to the rear of a rhododendron shrub that she found it. She stared for a while, made sure that nobody was looking her way, and then carefully lifted it, making sure to keep the roots covered in a ball of soil, and slipped it into her pocket. Nobody would miss a little plant like this, because nobody could have known that it was there. It would make a fantastic addition to her collection rather than being tossed into a compost heap as it surely would have been if anyone else had been weeding around that bush.

Elvira trimmed and nipped a few more plants, then they said their goodbyes, and headed to their respective cars in the parking lot.

"Are you going to stop over for a drink now that you don't have to stay home except for shopping?"

Donna smiled, grateful beyond words for what this woman had done for her with a few easy sentences. She was tired after all the excitement of the past couple of days though, and she wanted to get home as fast as she could to ensure the survival of her new plant. She shook her head.

"I'd love to come tomorrow if that's alright with you, but I want to get started with some planting today."

"Tomorrow is the wine and cheese evening for old people," Elvira said, with a wicked grin. "Now that really was pure fiction, so you can come and let your hair down finally, and know that that man of yours is not going to be looking for you, unless he wants to get embroiled in games of lawn bowls."

Chapter Twelve

Donna pushed her way between the towering shrubs behind the old farmhouse, shielding the young plants that she had taken from Lou's garden, now growing strongly in the plastic bag of nutrient rich soil that she'd had them in for the past few weeks. They were ready to go into the ground now, and it was time to take their places of pride in her special collection. It was only this morning, after discovering the twelfth of its kind beneath Lou's Rhododendron that she'd begun to wonder how they were getting there. But she had too much on her mind now to give it much thought.

Her life was changing fast. She took every opportunity to get out of the house now. She spent at least an hour of most weekdays in the gardens of the retirement homes, getting to know the residents and trying to help them in any way that they needed. She'd spent many an evening at Roses, and now was hesitantly sure that she finally had real friends. People who liked her. People who she was beginning to think just might have her back if she needed help. She was healing, and her resolve to leave was strengthening daily. She'd got to the point to where she almost didn't care what happened. She didn't think that Marco could legally just throw her out on the street, and she knew that he was unlikely to physically harm her.

She knew that as long as she stayed he could hurt her though. He was capable of thinking up very inventive ways to make her suffer. But even so, she'd lived in a state of such perpetual sadness, anxiety, and isolation for so many years, that her current fledgling awakening wasn't strong enough yet to stop whatever it was in her mind that instantly shut down thoughts of how to leave with floods of physical, brainless terror. Thinking things through was harder than she could ever have imagined. Still, she wanted more than anything to leave Marco. Many of the books she'd been reading contained accounts of people who still loved the narcissist psychos in their lives. Maybe they just hadn't stayed long enough. She knew that if you stayed long enough with one of these demons, you'd grow to know what true hatred is.

Marco wasn't liking the new Donna. It was obvious that it was making him extremely angry watching her come and go every day. Watching her get calls on her previously silent phone. She knew that he was perfectly capable of ruining everything for her, even if that meant that he'd never get to meet Elvira's fabulously rich father. She was finding it hard pretending that she was the still the same person she had been the day before she'd read the book that had shown her exactly what he was, but even though she still wasn't strong enough to figure out what to do, she was plenty strong enough not to allow his nastiness to affect her as it used to. She was sure that he'd make something happen soon to stop her slipping from his control, something nasty or outrageous.

She pushed through the shrubs in the grove she'd planted not too long after she realised that Marco never would consider crossing the terraces. When she'd realised that this place would be hers alone. She came to the landscaped clearing that was her favourite place to be in her world. Breathing in the peaty smell of the wild forest that surrounded and protected this place with its closely growing trees, she raised her face to the warmth of the sun, the peace of nature filling her entirely, leaving no space in her body for tension and terror. She walked around the clearing, inspecting all of her special plants, growing so abundantly, as if this was their natural environment. Smiling and at peace, she caressed a bloom here, stroked a leaf or two and made sure that the soil was still damp from her last watering. She planted her new babies into their new home and grunted with satisfaction, having a final look around. Papaver Somniferum, Mycelium Psilocybin lurking in the warm moist shade beneath an old hollow trunk, Jimbson, Lophophora Williamsii, Peyote, Erythoxylum, Catha Edulis, Tabernanthe iboga. And now this one. This little one made her collection of the most misunderstood of the healers finally complete.

*

Pretence and dishonesty were completely alien to her nature, but as she sliced mushrooms to go with the pasta she was making for supper, she found herself wondering how she could prolong this period of peace, so that she could think of a way out of the mess she was in without some terrible Marco originated pain. She hadn't realised before the books, but now she did know that the small or large dramas and discomforts he inserted into her life daily was done purposely to make sure she remained in a state of constant anxiety, probably to ensure her confused gratitude for those few times that he stopped. Even though she knew it, it still didn't make it easier to get a grip on herself when he was around. Enough of a grip to think things through properly at any rate. She couldn't yet see what she could do, but she knew that it would have to be something she did herself. Imposing herself on someone else wasn't an option. She poured stock on to the mushrooms in the pot, gathered up notebook, pen, and a glass of wine and settled down on the couch, determined to make a list of things that she needed to do to leave.

She wrote "Get a job", and then "Move Out", and could think of nothing beyond that. She couldn't commute from here to Wilson Springs every day and still get a day's work done. The drive was simply too long. And Marco would never allow her to work anyway while she was with him, even though he delighted in making sure that everyone knew how lazy she was. Moving out required somewhere to go to, and money. She didn't have enough money to pay for a place to stay. The thought of asking Elvira if she could stay there without any idea of how she could support herself made her cringe with shame. She ripped out the page, trembling, terrified of stepping out into the world after thirty years of being nothing, then hearing Marco's car, ran to the kitchen to throw it away. She was dressing the coleslaw when he came through.

"What did you do today," he asked abruptly.

"Just some weeding for Miss Lou and planted a couple of seedlings for Mr Gardner."

"Miss Lou," he sneered. "When did we teleport to the old South? What about Mr Young? Any sign of him?"

Donna thought fast, before turning around and smiling at him. "Oh yes," she said. "Elvira mentioned that he's very keen to make a trip around the old people's gardens. Soon. I'm sure it will be soon."

Marco's sour expression didn't change as he looked her up and down.

"What's with the face paint, and where did you get that slutty dress?"

She bit back the words that she wanted to say, and instead looked down at her dress.

"You bought it for me Marco," she murmured. "Shortly after we married. And I don't have any more makeup on than I usually wear."

He grunted, looking down at her as if she was a bit of crap on his shoe. "Yeh? Well maybe now you're a little old to be wearing it, don't you think? You already have the old lady crazies. People must be laughing at you. Maybe this going out all the time is a bad idea," he said, turning to leave. "This isn't a hotel where you get to come and go as you please."

As she set the plates on the table, she heard him rev his car and speed out of the driveway. She didn't bother to walk out of the door to make sure she'd heard correctly. She sat down and put her head in her hands, so tired of not knowing what was going to happen next. Tired of constantly being on edge not knowing what Marco was doing or would do. It was amazing how easily he still could cut her down. Bring her to her knees with a casual sentence. Obviously he still could, because she felt exactly like the bit of crap that his expression had conveyed that he was seeing. She checked to see that the stove was off, put the salads in the fridge, and went to bed.

*

He was in his study when she was woken by thunderous rain on the roof in the morning. Walking past, surprised that the door was open, she looked in to see him leaning back in his chair talking animatedly on the phone. She hurried down the passage, not wanting to hear what he was saying. There was a missed call from Elvira on her phone, which she'd left on the kitchen table. She deleted it. She felt totally miserable again, that old familiar painful, hopeless, desolate sadness filling her whole being. Lately she seemed to be bouncing between ecstatic hopeful joyfulness and utter devastation. It was exhausting. She didn't feel like talking to anyone at all. There was nothing she could do to make herself feel better. Or to make her life better. She made a cup of coffee and took it back up with her to her room to dress. Pulling on the tracksuit that she had mostly worn before Elvira had changed her life, she smiled bitterly. Before she'd met her she hardly ever made any sort of effort with her appearance. Days used to go by where she never bathed, changed or brushed her hair or teeth. She hadn't cared, and it was easier that way. Marco saved his jibes for when she did make an effort to look decent. She glanced in the mirror as she passed it. Mascara from yesterday smudged the skin beneath her eyes, and her hair was all over the place. She sighed and headed back downstairs. Marco was almost hysterically cheerful when he came into the kitchen for his breakfast.

"I'll be away for six weeks," he said. "Jackie has just got us our biggest client ever. I'll be flying out today to go over their requirements and finalise the deal, and then we have to tour all their facilities in Europe."

Donna stared at him. Jackie. His accountant. His lover. She had just got him his biggest client ever? His *accountant?* These weeks away had happened often before, although never before more than two weeks at a time. Then there'd always be some ridiculous reason to follow as to why every single one of these so called deals had supposedly fallen through. The questions bounced around her head, even though she knew very well that there would never be any point in voicing them. She knew that there was no client. She knew that he was going away somewhere wonderful with his lover. And it hurt. And it was terrifying. And he knew that it was. He liked her to be terrified.

She shivered. Her newfound knowledge told her that he was either doing this to make her jealous and get her back onto his crazy train of her destruction, or he she had stopped supplying what he needed, and he was about to throw her out. Even though what he was doing hurt, she wasn't jealous. Just cut to the core that she was so completely worthless as a human being that anyone could treat her this way. And even though she wanted more than anything to be away from him, to never see him again ever in her life, the lack of knowing how he intended to discard her was more frightening than if he'd thrown a sack of live snakes in her face.

He shovelled the last of his toast into his mouth, chewing like a chipmunk, the way he always did. She couldn't remember what it felt like to think he was handsome. Looking at the sour, self righteous face opposite her, all she could see now was disgusting. Pushing himself away from the table, he took his wallet out and tossed a few notes in front of her.

"That should do," he said, and then he left. She listened to him swear as he dragged his luggage down the stairs, and to the fading engine of his car, then she counted the money on the table. If she wanted to eat more than vegetables from her garden she would have to break into her secret little stash of savings. She shook her head, lead in her belly and ice running up her arms. Marco didn't know about her vegetable garden. She only grew herbs and a few ornamental chillies and cherry tomatoes above the terraces. He didn't care if she went hungry or if she had a medical emergency while he was gone.

Chapter Thirteen

Donna walked around the silent house, stopping now and then to pick up an ornament, or to touch the fabric of a curtain. All of these things that they'd acquired over the years meant nothing at all. Nobody else ever got to see them, and nothing was special. There had been no warm moments with friends and family to imbue any of their possessions with fond memories. Her daughter had been sent away as soon as he could manage it, and they weren't close. Always the spectre of Marco and the things he had done, or left undone, loomed between them. Her garden didn't seem so special now. Just the result of the desperate actions of a lonely woman. An unloved woman. A woman who meant nothing at all to anyone, filling the hours of her life with plants, and accidentally creating something of beauty. Something that nobody other than herself would ever get to see. Her existence – all of the years of her life had been totally, utterly, pointless. All the trying to understand her marriage. All the years of pretending. All for nothing. So what if she ended her life sleeping under a tree. There was no reason to try any more. She'd been stupid these last few weeks, thinking that she could get away. Have a normal life again. Stupid. All she'd ever have would be this, until Marco found a way to get rid of her when he was ready for that. The depression that had settled over her seemed to have physical weight to it now. She needed to sit down. She went back to the kitchen and just sat there, staring at the wall, ignoring the rings and beeps emanating from her phone. She didn't know what to do to fix herself. Or her life. So she sat.

*

They arrived just as the sun began to slip behind the mountains. She heard the cars in the drive, but didn't have the interest or the energy to get up. She heard the front door open, and the shuffling steps of several people talking softly.

"Anyone home?" called Elvira.

She stared wide-eyed as they came into the kitchen. Elvira, Sandy, Saul, and Laurence. Laurence. The last person in the world she wanted to see her this way. They looked around the darkening room, and then down at her, sitting at the table in her tatty clothing, hair wild, and the running black mascara beneath her eyes making them look huge, like a deer staring into headlights. Nobody said a word for quite a while, but their confusion and concern were evident. Donna moved her gaze to the table top. She didn't want their pity.

The light was switched on. "Is Marco around?" asked Elvira brightly.

Donna shook her head. "No. He won't be around for six weeks."

"Well then," said Elvira. "Cause for celebration. How about a drink for your travel weary guests?"

Donna stared fixedly at the table, wishing they would all go away. Hoping that if she ignored them totally they would. Instead she heard cupboard doors opening and closing, and then the clink of glasses and the bottles of wine in the fridge. She listened to them arranging themselves around the table and looked down at Laurence's hand pushing a glass of chilled white wine under her nose. She was accustomed to being embarrassed. She'd been regularly embarrassed over the years, but she couldn't recall ever feeling the shame she felt now. She was frozen to the spot.

"Nice kitchen," said Sandy. "I love all the little pots of herbs on the windowsill."

"Hmm," said Saul. "Must look wonderful with the sun coming through."

"I've got an orchid on my kitchen window," said Elvira.

"Yes," said Laurence. "But your kitchen windowsill is never visible behind all the sacks of flour and potting soil with cats on top."

"At least it's not decorated with bits of computer," said Elvira.

"That's just temporary," said Laurence.

Donna listened to the inane conversation, trying hard to stop the out of control laughter at this ridiculous situation from bubbling out.

"I truly hope so," said Sandy. "I need the files from that laptop. There must be more than twenty stories on it halfway to being books."

"I'm thinking of getting a kitten," said Saul.

"I like cats," said Laurence.

Donna looked up, runny mascara and dandelion hair forgotten. She wasn't sure how, but their conversation about nothing in particular had calmed her. It was hard to hang on to her misery in the midst of warm friendly people. Real people, enjoying their lives and each other.

"*There* you are," said Sandy. "Have you got any nibbles? I'm starving."

Donna nodded, and hastily left the room, running up the stairs to her bathroom to clean up her face and brush her hair. She looked in the mirror and still only saw ugly, but she didn't feel as close to dying of sadness as she had an hour ago. She rushed back down, stopping at her supply cupboard to grab bags of nuts and tortilla chips. They were still talking in the roundabout way that was their habit, bouncing comfortably between topics the way old friends do. She put the snacks into bowls on the table, and took a deep breath and a gulp of cold wine. She looked at Elvira.

"Why did you come?"

"You didn't answer your phone. I got worried. Under the circumstances—."

Donna blushed, getting angry now. It wasn't anyone's choice but her own who she chose to share her circumstances with, and now she deeply regretted talking to Elvira about it if she was going to share her private business with whoever she felt like. She glared at her, and looked from face to face at those around the table, trying to gauge if there was pity or disgust on any of them.

"What did you tell—?"

"There's no reason for anger my dear," said Saul. "Elvira said nothing other than that she was taking a drive out to you, and we insisted on coming with. That's a long, dark, road for a lady to drive on her own, and we thought we could have a fun visit with you. Maybe see your lovely gardens. We never knew that there was a problem."

"Until we arrived we didn't know, that is," said Sandy. "Obviously there *is* a problem."

Donna shook her head, anger gone as quickly as it had arrived, and shame back in firm control.

"You don't have to talk about it if you don't want to," said Elvira. "We've been friends long enough now for you to know that we care about each other. About you. We've been together every day for long enough for you to have decided whether or not to trust us."

Laurence topped up their glasses, and said, "That probably would depend on what the problem is Elvira. Sometimes sharing your problems, even with people who care, can seem like the hardest thing in the world to do."

"True enough," said Sandy. "I didn't trust any of you buggers enough to tell you all my dirty secrets until I'd known you for at least three days."

They all laughed, and Donna relaxed.

"We're all misfits you know," said Saul. "But we're there for each other. Always. We're family now. And so are you."

They sat around the table, drinking wine, and talking about everything under the sun except Donna. No one questioned her, and she realised now that they wouldn't ever try to force her, and also that if she did choose to talk about it, they wouldn't mock or ridicule her. But she wasn't ready to share her problems with anyone else, and she wasn't sure that she ever would be. The final words on the subject were spoken by Laurence.

"Think of these coming weeks as a holiday Donna," he said, looking into her eyes as though he knew everything. As though her wellbeing was important to him. "A time to organise your thoughts, and relax your body."

When they finally said their goodbyes after getting her promise that she would help put up a new trellis for Miss Lou the following day, she checked that all the doors were locked and went back to her kitchen.

This time when the nebulous fear started, and the worrying about what Marco would do next, she clenched her jaw and forced it out of her mind. She thought instead about the warm camaraderie around her table tonight, and the feeling of finally belonging somewhere squashed that cold anxiety, and replaced it with the warm glow of genuine affection.

She washed the wineglasses and snack bowls, and then curled up on the sofa and fell asleep watching When Harry Met Sally.

Chapter Fourteen

Laurence was already there when she arrived at Lou's, his large frame comically overflowing one of her delicate armchairs. Miss Lou was transferring the pies and pastries that he'd brought for her from Elvira into the little freezer compartment of her fridge. Elvira always made much too much, Donna guessed on purpose, and deliveries of extra food from the coffee shop and the catering business were made every day to the homes. Laurence and Saul took any of them who wanted to go into town to shop twice a week. They were good people, her new friends. All of them.

He smiled up at her and nodded, his mouth currently full of peanut butter biscuits. She smiled back. Over the past few weeks of working close to all the members of the group of friends, she had come to realise that Laurence wasn't anything like Marco at all. He was warm, funny, and kind, and seemed completely unaware of his startling good looks. His appearance didn't seem to mean anything to him at all if some of his outfits were anything to go by.

Donna accepted her tea and obligatory biscuits, and sat down to chat for a while before getting started on the trellis. Miss Lou always said that it was the highlight of her day when the young people came to call, being as she was, surrounded by senile geriatrics. The way she talked about her neighbours gave the impression that they were a lot older than she. Even though she was the oldest resident there, and physically in a bad way, she had the sharp wit of the well travelled, intelligent woman that she was, and a ribald sense of humour that very often made Donna laugh so hard that she cried a little. She was very fond of Miss Lou.

Lou followed them out, telling them about the time she had been the prima ballerina for a famous troupe in France, and wooed by an Italian prince. Donna envied her life of happiness and love a little, but then she thought about where that life would end, alone and forgotten in an old age home, and felt guilty for her envy. She would make sure that she did as much as she could to make sure that Miss Lou didn't get too lonely.

They worked in silence, comfortable with each other, until the trellis was up and secure, and then Laurence went out to his car to fetch one of the climbing miniature roses Miss Lou loved so much to plant against it. Donna wandered around the small garden, pulling an occasional weed and deadheading the patch of petunias. She looked behind the Rhododendron purely from habit, not expecting to see anything there again. But there they were. Three more. She checked to make sure that Miss Lou wasn't watching her, then eased the small plants from the soil and slipped them into her pocket.

Miss Lou kissed them both on both cheeks, and gave them each a mint humbug, then Donna followed Laurence's old Toyota to the coffee shop. She wondered what to do about the plants. One or two could be coincidence, but not as many as there had been. She decided reluctantly that she would have to show them to Elvira. Something odd was going on.

*

Donna leaned back into her favourite overstuffed couch, the one that made her feel as though her whole body was being hugged, and watched her new friends talking, typing, and Saul doing a sketch of her. She wasn't self-conscious with any of them at all anymore, and even though he had been staring at her on and off for the past hour it didn't bother her. She was waiting for Elvira to go to the kitchen, and when she did, she hurried after her.

"I found something in Miss Lou's garden," she said, taking the wilted plants out of her pocket and holding them out on her palm. "Under the Rhododendron."

Elvira looked down, expressionless and silent. She looked closely, for a very long time. Finally Donna guessed that she didn't know what she was looking at. And why would she? These weren't your common garden plants.

"They're Cannabis Sativa," she said. "Marijuana. Weed. Pot."

Elvira looked up sharply, tried to purse her lips, and then laughed explosively. Donna assumed it was the shock. Eventually when she stopped laughing, Elvira took a tissue from her pocket, blew her nose and wiped her eyes. She looked into Donna's eyes with a smile, and took the plants from Donna's hand.

"Secrets," she said. "We've been keeping secrets. Just like you my lovely Donna. Come. Maybe the time for all our secrets is over."

Donna frowned and followed her back out. Elvira strolled over to Saul, who was engrossed in his picture of Donna. She put her hand between his face and his sketchpad. He also stared for quite a while before looking up.

"They were growing under Miss Lou's Rhododendron," she said. "Donna found them."

Everyone strolled over to inspect Elvira's palm.

"Well," said Saul. "We'd better tell her what they are then."

"She knows what they are," said Elvira.

"It's Mr Hyde," said Laurence. "It's the seeds. He will insist on rolling his outside, even though I've told him that if the management find out the party will be over for all of us." He looked at Donna.

"Fortunately he always does it in the same place, so I thought I'd got them all."

Donna was flabbergasted. What was going on here? Were they selling drugs to the elderly under the guise of helping them with their gardens?

Sandy chuckled. "You look so shocked. Come sit, and we'll tell you."

She took hold of Donna's elbow and led her back to the seats. Drinks were topped up, Elvira went back to the kitchen to get the snacks she had wanted to fetch before Donna had interrupted her, and they all settled back down and started to explain.

"The retirement homes we help don't offer much, other than the rental of those little flats. The communal recreational areas are free for the old people to use, but the canteens and chemists are basic, and most of those folk don't have a lot of money," said Elvira. "Most of them don't see loved ones very often, if at all, and there are many with incredible pain and health issues."

"So we help a couple of them out with a little natural remedy for free," said Saul.

"Pot?" Donna raised a brow, not sure where she stood as far as supplying illegal drugs to anyone at all. Her little collection of illegal plants was a different thing altogether. She grew them for the botanical treasures that they were. She never got high on them, and would never dream of giving them to anyone else to get high on either. "Where do you get it?"

"Saul knows where to buy it safely," said Elvira. "And it's paid for with funds from the Gardens for Grandparents. There's no shortage of cash, thanks to my father. We banked the lump sum he gave, and the monthly interest from that is plenty to help the old folk in all sorts of ways."

Donna didn't doubt the medicinal potency of Cannabis. In fact, she knew a lot about many medicinal plants and their uses, and she herself wasn't exactly an angel when it came to following the laws of the land. Ninety percent of her special garden had been built from stolen cuttings from various public or private gardens, and if she was ever found out she could find herself in quite a lot of trouble. But she was very unlikely to be found out because her gardens were so well hidden. Thoughts raced through her mind. Imagining herself being arrested gave her chills. So did the visions of Marco's possible reactions. Her first instinct was to run away. She had more than enough problems of her own. But the thought of leaving this small group of people who had come to mean so much to her produced an actual physical pain in her heart. She knew that her life was about to change for better or worse soon, and even though the thought of change terrified her, the thought of losing them scared her just as much.

"Good," she said, nodding her head.

"You're alright with this?" Laurence sounded more than a little surprised.

She nodded. "I think that it would probably be a much better idea to supply them with cannabis oil though, rather than have them smoke it."

"Cannabis of any kind is illegal here," said Saul. "So even though we could easily buy the oil, it would be way too risky to bring it in. And they don't all smoke it. Quite a few of them brew it up as a tea."

"I could probably make some if I had enough of the raw material to work with," said Donna. "In fact, I know I could make some. I've extracted oils from plants before. It's not at all difficult."

Elvira laughed. "Hopefully one day Donna will introduce us to her own collection of plants. She knows more about horticulture than any of us Sunday gardeners Laurie, and she's no stick in the mud either."

"Sounds intriguing."

They spent a while discussing medicinal plants, and she found herself wanting to share knowledge that she had. She wanted to share the secrets that she had kept to herself for over twenty years with these people, and without giving it much thought she gave in to the impulse.

"I'll show you," she said. "I trust all of you, so I'll show you my special garden."

Then the conversation moved to darker topics, when Sandy asked her about the state they'd found her in.

"You're obviously having some trouble," she said. "Serious trouble. Do you trust *us* enough yet to tell us about it? Is it your husband?"

Donna blushed, not sure what to say, but finally really wanting to get it out of her. She did want to tell them now, but the fears of either ridicule or pity loomed large in her mind.

"My husband dumped me," said Sandy. "Quite abruptly. If it wasn't for these three people here I don't know what I would have done."

"You're well rid of him," said Laurence, face grim. "He treated you like a doormat. You were a wreck when he left you, but look at you today. Successful, confident, and happy."

Donna listened in silence for a while. Listened to the stories of almost wasted lives, jealousy, hatred, and pain inflicted by those who were supposed to love you the most, and she wondered if they had all been burned by narcissists. Such similar stories with the hurts they had had. Surely there couldn't be so many around? Eventually she told them, after they'd shared their darkest secrets with her. How could she not trust them after they had bared their own souls? Talking about her life wasn't easy, because she still was unsure if she had imagined most of what Marco had done. They listened, and asked questions, and in the end they insisted that she wasn't crazy, and insisted too that she must leave the devil that she was with.

"Seems like the universe has gathered a little group of the ex-victims of these creatures together Donna," said Elvira. "Maybe just for you. We all seem to have been there one way or another, but we all escaped, even those of us who wanted to stay and thought that our hearts would break when we were discarded. Look at all of us now my friend, and *know* that you will escape too. We found each other, and now you've found us."

When Elvira reached across and squeezed her hand, Donna squeezed back, knowing that she had found home. Whether it was the universe or some other power that had conspired to bring her here didn't matter anymore, but she doubted that coincidences could ever be this happy. This right. She'd found her people, even though they weren't the sort of people you would mostly find.

*

And so she showed them all her secrets. Marco had been away for three weeks without any attempt to contact her, when Donna first noticed how different she felt now without him around. As if some painful constriction of her whole self had been lifted from her. She was enjoying herself. Laughing and having fun. She took pride in her appearance every day again, and she was loving the care that she was now giving only to herself, and her body. Her friends came and went

127

regularly, spending time with her in her gardens, especially the one that had been seen by her eyes only for so long. They helped her clean the stills, and marvelled at the healthy crop of cannabis they'd be able to harvest for the oil. She was in her element, and all the knowledge that she had gained over the years came to the fore, and she was liberally bathed in their admiration. That garden blooming with health, and consisting of some of the rarest plants on the planet, as well as every single one on the list of illegal plants to own in the country. She showed them how to make teas, tinctures, creams and powders, and they had started taking some of these to the old people.

Donna was filled with happiness, comfortable in her own skin, and finally proud of the knowledge and abilities she possessed, she had begun to see a light at the end of the tunnel. She felt useful now. There was purpose to her life, and all she had to do was find out how her talents could get her away from Marco forever. With three more peaceful weeks to go she believed she had a chance to figure something out.

Chapter Fifteen

Laurence and Saul were helping her put up stakes for her heirlooms. She'd been startled when they'd offered. Donna did everything around the house herself. She'd long ago given up asking Marco for help. He either couldn't, or wouldn't, do a single thing. When he was home, he was either watching television or in his study. He did go out of his way to irritate her though, always making sure to do the little things he knew she hated. She'd stopped thinking that he was just forgetful right after she'd tripped and fallen in the supermarket, and he had stood there with a small smile, looking down on her as she struggled to her feet on her own. She'd realised then that her husband would never willingly help her with anything. Not even if she fell down. Remembering that gleeful, avid, sparkle in his eye when she was hurt or humiliated made her sick. Donna could do most things that men generally did around family households, and she never asked anyone for anything.

"And we're done," said Saul, standing up straight and looking down the straight row of stakes and cross stakes.

"Now that just looks great. Even if I do say so myself," said Laurence.

Donna looked at him, standing in the sun, the affectionate twinkle in his eye that seemed to be reserved only for her, and the smile that brought the dimple to the side of his lips. She'd developed a very soft spot for Laurence.

"I can't thank both of you enough," she said. "It would've taken me ages without your help."

"That's what friends are for love," said Saul, throwing an arm around her shoulders, and giving her a squeeze.

Glowing from the unaccustomed feeling of another human's friendly touch, she led the way to the main house and heated up the lasagne she had made in anticipation of them coming today, while they washed the soil off as best they could. She had broken into her saved cash, and bought a couple of bottles of wine and the ingredients for a strawberry cream pie to go with it, not a crumb of which was left at the end of the meal.

"You're a fantastic cook," said Saul. "I haven't eaten so well in years."

Laurence nodded. "A gorgeous gardener, and she cooks like an angel too," he said.

Donna didn't take compliments very well. She didn't believe them very much, but these past few weeks she had realised that none of her new friends said anything other than what they genuinely felt. It was so uplifting interacting with nice people after forgetting what they were for so long.

"Thank you," she said.

They both helped her clear the table, but she insisted that the dishes be left for her to do later. They'd done enough work for one day.

"I have to be going," said Saul, checking his watch. "Are you going to follow me Laurie?"

Laurence shook his head. "I'll leave in a bit, if that's alright with you Donna. I was hoping to swipe a couple of cuttings from your patio first."

"Of course," said Donna, suddenly feeling hugely uncomfortable at the thought of being alone with him, but saying no would have been churlish after all he had done to help her. Thinking about Marco's reaction if he were to ever find out that these men had been on his property all day, and eaten at his table gave her chills. Marco didn't think that she was attractive to other men in any way, but he was big on ownership rights.

They stood side by side watching Saul's tail lights disappear down the drive, and then went to the patio to snip the cuttings he wanted. When they were finished, he said, "Can I stay a while? I've been wanting to talk to you, but we always seem to be in a crowd."

She stared up at him, alarmed now, needing to get him out as fast as she could.

"Don't," he said, his own expression pained at the look of terror on her face. "I won't so much as come within a metre of you. I promise. I wouldn't ever hurt you. I just want to talk."

She turned away from him and took several deep breaths, before she managed to push the panic down. She knew that he would be true to his word. Her husband might be a lying, cheating, soul vampire, but Donna lived true to her own morals, and she would never cheat on him as long as she lived with him as his wife. The thought that she was somehow cheating on Marco just by spending some time alone with Laurence loomed in her mind now, but she turned, smiling brightly. Falsely.

"Of course you can," she said. "We'll have another glass of wine."

Sitting back at the table seemed safest to her, and she made sure that she was on the opposite side of it after he sat down. He opened the bottle of red wine between them, and filled their glasses. They sipped silently for a long while. Eventually she settled down completely, back to feeling safe and cared for, as she always did in this man's company.

"Why don't you wear a wedding ring?"

She was about to ask him why he wanted to know, but then she realised that she wanted to tell him. The shame of her life was always with her, but she knew that he would never mock her with anything she shared with him. She told him the truth. The conversation started awkwardly, but when she noticed again, the wine was finished, and she had told him almost everything. So much more than she'd originally shared with the group of friends. When she looked up, she realised with a shock that his eyes were brimming. He seemed to be fighting back tears. Then he went to the bathroom and she was sure that she must have imagined it.

"I'd better be getting home," he said. "I've got a couple of websites to tweak."

She got up to walk him out, but he stood where he was, so she waited.

"We need to talk some more Donna," he said. "And there's something I want to show you. Tomorrow. Will you meet me at Charly's at around ten?"

"What do you want to show me?"

He laughed, melting her heart with his dimple. "Nothing dangerous. Trust me Donna. I meant it when I said I would never do anything to hurt you."

"Fine then," she said, smiling up at him. "Tomorrow at ten it is."

He wouldn't let her walk him to his car as she was about to do. He looked out into the darkness, knowing that this was the only inhabited building in a twenty mile radius, and was unable to stop the anger from showing on his face. He shook his head.

"You lock up," he said. "I'll go after I've heard that big old padlock click home."

She stood looking down at the padlock for some time after the rumbling of his car engine faded into the distance, remembering the raging of her husband when he'd come home from one of his absences to find that she'd fitted it herself. He'd screamed about how crap it looked on the expensive wooden door, and he'd screamed some more about who the hell did she think she was trying to lock him out of his own house. Sharing her fear of being alone so often at night, so far away from civilisation had brought only laughter.

"You're such a little coward," he had said. "Nobody's interested in breaking down doors to get to *you*."

How odd it was to have someone care whether she lived or died. Smiling, she wrapped her arms around her waist, wanting to keep the warm glow that nestled beneath there now, forever.

Chapter Sixteen

Donna left early to drop a few containers of herbal medicines at Rainbow Acres, and got waylaid by Elvira who was rearranging a garden for a new tenant. Elvira smiled broadly at her and gave her a small hug.

"You're looking so much brighter now that your husband isn't around. You just remember what I said. You come and stay with me till you find your feet. Don't stay with that asshole a minute more."

"Thank you," she said. "I might just take you up on that. Soon."

"Good," said Elvira. "Saul says that you're a better cook than I am. The swine. I could use some help at the coffee shop though. Your lasagne and pie sound delicious."

"I don't cook better than you. That's just Saul stirring."

"Still," Elvira said. "I've been leaning towards making medicinal brownies for Mr Hyde until we can get the first batch of oil. Sooner or later one of the management is going to find one of those special little weeds and it will ruin everything for all of them. Not to mention getting the lot of us arrested. They need us, and I don't want to jeopardise what we can do to help them. As it is there are rumours flying around that the owners are thinking of selling. I can only hope that they're not true."

Finally, after promising to make the brownies, Donna managed to extricate herself and arrived at Charly's a few minutes after ten. Laurence was sitting at a window. He smiled and waved when he saw her.

"I'm so sorry," she said, softly telling him about Elvira and the brownies. "I'm never late."

He grinned at her. "I am. Quite a lot."

She laughed. Laurence had to be the easiest person in the world to be with. He ordered coffees and they chose a few different varieties of pastries to share.

"So what's this thing you want to show me?"

"It's not too far away," he said. "You can follow me if you don't feel safe with me driving you."

"I don't have to follow you," said Donna straight away. "What is it though? Will you give me a clue?"

Laurence looked out of the window for a while. "All that you told me last night." He turned and looked at her, his expression unreadable. "I knew someone who lived pretty much the same way you have up till now. Maybe worse. Or maybe not so much worse as just a different kind of the same. If you know what I mean. What you've had has been bad beyond belief, but for her—. She lived that way till the end though. I want to show you what that could mean. What it could mean if you don't leave."

Donna's stomach lurched, at a total loss for words, she simply nodded. Deftly, Laurence changed the subject, whispering different ideas for special cakes other than brownies, each one crazier than the last. By the time he held the passenger door of his car open for her she was laughing again.

Music came on when he started the engine. Mr Bojangles. She looked at him, eyebrow quirked, but he just grinned, turned it up and sang along, totally off key. She wound down her window, the warm breeze ruffling her hair and caressing her cheeks was filled with the scents of summer and life. Marco's driving always scared her stiff. He was always making such an effort to look good that he drove too fast, and was constantly looking at himself in the rear view mirror. Funny in a cliché kind of way, but still terrifying for a passenger. This car was solidly on the tar and under Laurence's control. She looked at him out of the corner of her eye, still singing with a silly grin on his face, and realised that there was no place in the world that she would rather be than here with him. Wistfully, she briefly allowed herself to imagine what life would have been like with a man like him, but then quickly stopped those thoughts from growing. It was pointless mourning what could have been, when nothing could be done to change what was.

She looked around at the houses they were driving past. They were in the old affluent part of town, where the houses were all huge mansions, and mostly empty now, their owners preferring to live closer to modern life. Laurence reached over and put the music off before stopping at a gate nestled in high walls, and digging for the remote to open it. The drive was long, and it was only after rounding a sharp bend in the avenue of tall trees that the house became visible. Donna's eyes widened at the sight. Four stories high, it had wings and turrets, and small leaded windows above the eaves. White marble columns flanked the front doors, and statuary and topiaries finished the effect of a truly stately home.

"Wow," she said. "Who lives here?"

"Nobody lives in the main house now," he said, parking on the immaculate lawn and pulling the key from the ignition. "I live in the guest house around the back."

"So who—?"

"It's mine," he said. "Come. I'll show you."

Donna followed him into the house through the tall front doors which opened smoothly considering their size. It was obviously well maintained and cared for. The hallway stretched to the left and right, glistening Italian marble covering the floor. Large Persian carpets scattered here and there looked like small throw rugs in the huge space. A broad single stairway led up to sunshine streaming through the bay windows on the first floor, where it branched off once again, left and right.

They walked silently through so many rooms Donna lost count. Rooms of such size and filled with such opulence that she couldn't begin to imagine to value of such a place. Finally they reached the very top floor. Small rooms that must have housed the servants back in the days when this house was new. Laurence led her into the final room at the end of the long passage. A neatly made bed in the corner, a bedside table and two chairs were the only furnishings. Laurence walked over to the small window, and beckoned. She went to stand beside him, slightly queasy looking down. Donna was petrified of heights.

"My mother," he said. "Jumped from this window. That's how she died."

She gasped, but could think of not a single word to say. He walked over to the bed and sat down. Donna sat in the ancient armchair, and waited for him to continue.

"I'd moved out by then," he said. "Rather I should say, I'd been kicked out by then. You'd think that anyone living in such a house would be happy."

He looked over at her with a rueful smile. "But I learned early that houses don't make you happy. People do."

"I'm sorry," she said.

"The man you described to me last night. Your husband. He could be a clone of my father. Except for the violence that is. My father had no problems with beatings. I think he enjoyed them to be honest. He beat me regularly. And her. My mother. He also took any excuse to smack the staff around when he knew that he could get away with it. He always hated me. My first memories are of getting slapped just for playing with my mother. Eventually my mother stopped paying me any attention at all when he was around. But when he wasn't, she was the sweetest woman in the world. The day I turned eighteen, he gave me a thousand dollars and told me to get out, and never to set foot in his house ever again. He didn't even try and supply a reason. He did me a favour actually. I think I might have killed him if I'd stayed."

He got up and strolled over to the window, looking down.

"I only saw my mother a few times after that. She'd pretend to go for a walk, and I'd meet her in the next street. But it terrified her so much, the thought of being found out by him, that I eventually stopped calling her. She had my number, but she very seldom called. Occasionally a hushed and hurried conversation, but that was it. I found out that she had died from the newspaper. And how she had died. He was killed shortly afterwards, by one of his lovers. If only she'd waited for a few short weeks before deciding to end her life."

"Oh Laurence," she said. "I can't imagine—."

He spun around sharply and sat back down on the bed, leaning forward staring into her eyes.

"Yes you can Donna," he said. "I know that you're stronger than she was, and that your Marco at least doesn't beat you black and blue, but after listening to you last night, I also know that you've plumbed the same depths of sadness that my mother did. She also believed that she had nowhere to go. She also pretended to the world that life was just rosy, and that she was happily married. She could have survived if she'd left him, but only up to a point in time. Somewhere along the line she lost some spark, that little remnant of individuality that remained, and after that I don't believe that she could have left even if someone had given her a million dollars."

"I don't understand."

He shook his head. "Last night, scattered in amongst the things you told me about Marco's behaviour, you also said quite a few other things. That you felt sorry for him. That you had loved him. That you wanted to forgive him. You made quite a few excuses for him."

"I did not!" Donna leapt out of her chair, scowling down at him.

He stood up and walked over to her. "Yes you did," he said softly. "Your staying is about more than a roof and a job Donna. He's been grooming you your whole adult life, and he's very happy with what he has created. You told me that you gave up after your breakdown. That you made a point of expecting nothing, and shutting yourself off from the things that had hurt you. You're terrified for terror's sake now, and until you begin to expect everything in the world for yourself, knowing that you deserve so much more than you have, and open yourself up to everything that's possible for you, you'll never be free of him, even if you do leave him. You have to stop believing that the way he has treated you – is treating you – is in any way acceptable. When he's charming, you melt, and forget about the bad times, convincing yourself that you were wrong about him. And as long as you live with him that's not going to stop, no matter what you think now. I know. My father could charm the gold out of your teeth when he wanted something. He used to have my mother smiling and laughing with him long before her bruises healed. Every time. She felt some kind of crazy comfort in the routine of her life, so she stayed, even though her life was horrible in every possible way. He killed her just as effectively as if he'd thrown her out of this window himself. In fact, I'm sure she died long before she took that leap. I don't want anything like that for you. You deserve infinitely better. If you need somewhere to stay, I'll help you, but you need to get out of that house."

"Stop Laurence," she said. "Please. Just stop." Her head was spinning. "I can't just walk away from thirty years. Like it never happened. There has to be an ending. An end. Something—." Hearing his words brought it all back. He was right. She burst into tears.

He put his arms around her, and held her till her sobs subsided. She didn't want to move. There was nothing remotely sexual in his embrace. She realised that this was what real men did. They gave comfort when it was needed in ways that meant something. This was what she wanted. Not being the outwardly thick skinned woman who was never touched, who never needed anything from anyone, but who craved love and affection even so. She wanted to be able to cry, or laugh, or say something affectionate without being ridiculed. She wanted to be held when she cried. She wanted to be held by someone who cared. Finally she pushed herself away from him and blew her nose.

"Sorry," she said.

"You don't have to be sorry with me Donna. Never."

"I don't know what to do," she said.

"How about I make you a cup of coffee?"

They walked back down through the silent house, but this time Laurence led her down a different staircase to the kitchen. Kitchens more than kitchen. She stopped in the middle of the largest of them, gazing around at the high walls with her mouth open.

"You actually lived here? Grew up here?"

"Yeah," he said, wrestling with the key to the door out to the back. "Trust me. As I said, life isn't about houses."

Finally he got the door opened, and she followed him out into the courtyard. There were outbuildings left and right. She recognised the stables, but the rest of them loomed mysteriously. They walked through an arch in a high stone wall, and once again she was astounded. A fairly modern swimming pool twinkled in the sunshine. Dark blue, with two waterfalls flowing busily into it from opposite ends. Here was where he'd created his garden, and it was starkly beautiful. She felt as though she had stepped through a magical portal straight into a royal garden in Japan, and insisted on walking through every part of it before having coffee. Finally they reached the cottage where he lived. It was sparsely furnished, but still warmly welcoming. The sliding doors they had entered through gave way to an open plan lounge and kitchen, and seeing the bits of his life scattered around gave her the urge to inspect them all. She smiled at the neat row of computer parts looking out of place on the kitchen window sill.

She sat, watching his back as he made coffee. He was a tall, well built man. He obviously looked after himself. With his handsome, chiselled features and the wonderful human being that he was, she wondered why he was alone. Curiosity got the better of her after he handed her a cup and sat down beside her.

"Have you never married?" she asked.

He shook his head.

"Because of your childhood? Your father?"

He laughed. "No," he said. "Not that. I believe in marriage. And love. I've seen lots of love in my time, including my childhood. It suited my father that I stayed out of his sight, so I spent the majority of my time with friends. Their parents and families saved me. They taught me what it was to be human, and to love and be loved. No. It wasn't my father. I've just never met anyone who I loved enough. And to be honest, I think that most of the women who went out with me did it more for the love of that house than me."

"Seems a shame. Standing empty like that."

"It's a cash vampire," he said. "I was surprised when I inherited it. I'm sure that if my father had realised he would die so soon, he would have made sure that it was left to anyone other than me. It probably never occurred to him that something as mundane as death could touch someone as wonderful as himself. He never bothered with what would happen to the people in his life after he died, so he never changed the will that he'd made out when my parents had first married. All his worldly goods left to her in the event of his death, and in the event of her death it all would go to their oldest surviving child if they had any. I was an only child, so there it was. Unfortunately there wasn't a lot of money left behind. It barely pays for the upkeep of the house. I should sell it. It's just—. My mother really loved that old house. The only truly happy memories I have of her was when she was showing me some new thing she had done to it or for it."

She smiled at him. "Sometimes houses do matter Laurence."

He drove her back to her car, and opened her door for her.

"Donna—," he said.

"What Laurence?"

"Nothing." He reached across and gently wiped her cheek with the back of his finger. "Just a bit of mascara there."

Chapter Seventeen

As she measured the dried cannabis powder into the rich brownie mix, Donna thought about what would happen when Marco came home. She'd been living her life as though she was single these past few weeks. With the support of her friends, knowing that they really would help her if need be, and that they would because they cared for her, her confidence had grown. She was able to think clearly most of the time now, hardly ever approaching that locked in, locked away place she used to exist in before. But when he came back, she knew that there would be no more visits from her friends. She wouldn't be able to spend as much time as she had been at the old farmstead in her gardens, and she knew that her almost daily drives into Wilson Springs would be stopped. She certainly wouldn't be able to bake special brownies in this kitchen. Now that she was out of the confused, disconnected state she'd been in, and realised just how insane her life had been until just a few weeks ago, she knew she had to decide what to do quickly. Before he returned. Because she wouldn't be able to hang on to her current equilibrium afterwards. She put the tins in the oven and went to fetch her laptop.

She searched for jobs in Wilson Springs. There were two. One for a waitress at Charly's, and another for a live in handyman. Then she searched for horticultural positions further afield, but they all required minimum years of hands on experience. She could move in with Elvira, but how would she pay her way? Baking a couple of batches of brownies wouldn't do the trick. Or she could take the help that Laurence offered. She wasn't sure what exactly it was that he had been offering. She couldn't live with him while she was still married to Marco. And even if she did, what would she do to survive. She had no intention of being a bum.

Depressed again, she idly googled the various medicinal herbs, searched holistic healing sites, and then suddenly it hit her. She could sell her herbal remedies online. Obviously not the illegal ones, but there seemed to be a lot of interest in natural medicines these days, and if there was one field that she was an expert in that was it. She jumped up excitedly, having to move around. To be mobile as she thought. She'd need more equipment eventually, but to begin with all she'd need would be containers, packing materials, and enough cash to ship orders out. And a website. She'd need a website. She couldn't afford to pay him yet, but if Laurence agreed to help her set one up, she would pay him when she could afford it. All the time she'd thought that she was useless and completely lacking in any ability, and thought of her gardening merely as an escape from her reality. But it was a talent. Something that she was not simply proficient at, but something that she knew inside and out. And she'd been learning all the time. Finally, she'd found her way out. She knew she could do this.

She spent the evening making lists, and digging out all of the old books she'd collected on the subject. She wasn't stupid enough to believe that she would make a fortune. She was fully aware that she'd have to work hard to succeed at this, but at least it was a beginning. Something to work towards, and she'd stay right here until she felt secure enough to leave. It was about time she got something out of her marriage, even if it was just food and accommodation on her own terms. She would have to pretend and lie just as well as her husband did. Suddenly a wave of guilt swept over her. She was being deceptive, dishonest, and thinking of using Marco even though she knew she planned on leaving him. Not to mention all the entertaining of men she'd been doing in his absence. And that embrace. Her face flushed and her heart swelled remembering Laurence's warm arms around her, and the knowledge that that's exactly where she wanted them to be made her squirm.

She shook herself. The time had come to be honest with herself. Marco had done nothing to earn her loyalty. He hadn't ever made her feel like a human being let alone make her feel truly loved. He hadn't cared whether she faltered and fell. She knew that he would, and had, engineered her falls. The only love in this marriage had come from her, and that had been a long time ago. In her mind and her heart, Marco was not her husband anymore. And she owed him no loyalty. She owed him nothing at all. And she'd take what she needed from him for as long as she needed to. If she was going to succeed in creating a business strong enough to feed and house herself for the rest of her life, she had a lot of hard labour ahead of her, but she was determined to do this. She made herself a cup of hot chocolate, and took it and her laptop to bed with her, totally exhausted, in the best kind of way.

*

Fuelled with inspiration, Donna woke early and drove to Roses to drop the batch of brownies off.

"That's a brilliant idea!" said Elvira. "You see? There's always a way out, no matter how difficult things seem to be."

"I'm thinking about maybe cultivating and selling plants and seeds too," said Donna. "I must find out more about shipping them though."

"Now that you know how you're going to earn your crusts, you can move in here with me straight away."

Donna shook her head, unable to quell the excitement of finally having a plan to leave, nor the fear of all the things that could go wrong until she did. "It's going to take at least a couple of weeks. I can't leave my gardens now. Once I know it's going to work, I'm

150

going to have to move the plants I'll be using for the business with me."

"We can start that right now," said Elvira. "Start getting them sorted, and bring them across here, and you can rest easy that they'll be looked after until you get here. I have a lovely secluded little spot that we can hide your special darlings away in."

Donna agreed, hope and joy filling her in ways that she could never have imagined. She rushed to town to get prices for plastic jars and containers to ship her products in, impatient to get started. She bought samples of each, as well as labels and wrapping paper, planning on packing one or two and then throwing them around to see how well they would fare on trips around the world.

Driving home, she impulsively put the radio on. This was something she hadn't done for years, because music made her sad mostly. But not this time. She hummed along to an old Foreigner song. She used to love all Foreigner's music. A few months ago, she had known for a fact that she would spend the rest of her life in that special kind of loneliness that Marco had given her. That she would die alone, and that nobody would care when she did. Now she thought that she might have a chance to spend however many years remaining to her living a meaningful life. Maybe even a life with love in it. Real love. The image of Laurence singing Mr Bojangles made her smile. She shook her head. No. It was too late for that kind of love. She was too old, and she could never put herself in a position where anyone could do to her what Marco had done again. Remembering how wonderful he had been in the beginning, she knew now how a seemingly perfect, loving angel could be the cleverly constructed exterior shell, concealing the vicious demon within, biding his time, waiting to crush you like a bug. Anyway. All that she and Laurence shared was the warm affection of friendship. Not love. She wasn't in his league.

Marco's car was in the drive, parked askew and blocking the garage doors. She turned the ignition off, and sat there, trying to collect herself. What was he doing here? He wasn't supposed to be home for three weeks. The constriction of her shoulder blades and the tremors in her body had started back up the instant she had seen the vehicle. The absence of the constant tension and fear that she had been so used to the past weeks made its sudden resurgence bring on a huge wave of anger. How could the mere proximity of another human being cause such pain and panic? She closed her eyes and willed her muscles to relax. It didn't work. Slowly she walked past the Bentley. The windscreen was shattered, and there were multiple dents in the bonnet. It looked like it had been pelted with rocks.

He was sitting at the kitchen table, eating a sandwich, wearing only a towel around his waist, and still damp from the shower. The sight of his half naked body revolted her. His previously muscular torso had disappeared and now a flabby paunch sagged towards his lap, his greed for all the luxuries in life finally catching up with him. He turned to her with a grin. His face was crisscrossed with scratches, and one of his eyes was a mere slit in swollen blue flesh.

"Hello," he said. "Busy with your grannies, are you?"

"Hi," she said, going with the flow. Marco's charm switch was at full volume. She wondered what crappy thing he had done this time. "Yes. There are a couple of new tenants with bare gardens who need help."

"Good, good," he said, stuffing the rest of his sandwich in his mouth. Donna watched him chew. Everything he did disgusted her now. She knew that he was mentally ill, with the thought processes of a spoiled three year old, but even her disgust didn't manage to quell the unreasonable fear he had instilled in her. She put the milk and bread that she had bought away, knowing that he was waiting for her to ask about the car and his face, but she couldn't allow him to see that she really didn't care. Whatever he told her would be a lie anyway. Right now she couldn't risk him knowing that she hated him, because she knew his revenge would be swift. Marco was capable of doing anything when it came to keeping her in line. Anything at all. He was supremely confident of his total control of her, of her adoration of him, and if she didn't ask he might wonder why.

"You had an accident," she said, giving him the lie she knew was coming.

"Just a little fender bender," he said. "Nothing for you to concern yourself with my darling."

She looked away. At this point in her life she couldn't be less concerned about him or him being hurt. What did concern her deeply was the over the top affection in his tone. And the use of the word darling. That one hadn't been dusted off in too many years to remember. Whatever he had done this time to warrant such a display of affection must be bad.

"Have you met Mr Young yet?" he asked.

She shook her head.

"Ask Elvira for his private number," he said, smiling a beguiling smile that clashed disturbingly with the coldness of his eyes. "I've tried to contact him through the obvious channels, but it's impossible. If she thinks you're her friend now, she'll give it to you. May as well use all our resources."

Donna nodded and turned to leave the room. Resources. He'd often used the term to describe his workers, and now it struck her that no normal human being would call a friend a resource. A person should never be seen as a resource. And Donna was her friend, in the true sense of the word. Marco couldn't see that. Marco probably wouldn't ever understand the concept of friendship. Lately many of the things he'd said over the years were popping up in her mind, and leaving her at a loss as to why she'd never picked up on them before. Maybe because she was becoming herself again. No. That wasn't right. She didn't honestly know who she was any more. She'd been the person that Marco had created for so long, and even though the shock of the realisation of what he was, and what he had purposely done to her had miraculously, almost instantly, shed the scales from her vision, she knew that finding herself again wasn't going to be a walk in the park. She knew that she was damaged. Deeply damaged. Soul damaged. Anyone who hadn't lived her life would have difficulty understanding that. It was a struggle for her to remember the woman she had been before Marco, and it was a struggle to know who she was now, outside of the chaos of her thoughts and emotions. She still wavered between knowing that he had hurt her on purpose, and wondering whether she was mistaken.

"Wait," he said. She stopped and started back to him.

"I've been thinking," he said. "Thinking of moving to another country soon. Australia maybe."

Taking a bucket of ice water to the face couldn't have produced a bigger shock. Was he finally going to leave her? Or was he planning on them leaving together? What about Shelley? She stared at him, not sure what to say. He often came out with expansive statements that almost knocked her senseless, and then never acted on them. But sometimes he did follow through with his crazy awful plans. He was quite capable of doing things that she could never imagine doing, and he had never asked for her opinions, wants, or needs before he did them. This time she watched the expressions on his face as her distress became visible in the quiver of her lip, and the trembling through her body. He grinned, obviously relishing the sight, greedily drinking in her anguish as if it fed him in some way.

And then the pain came. Something inside of her broke. Why did she keep thinking that her new knowledge had made her strong, and that he couldn't hurt her anymore? Marco would probably always have the power to hurt her in one way or another as long as he remained in her physical space. A deep ache that spread hotly through her core, and made her want to cry. To scream, and cry, and rage at the creature she'd thought was the love of her life, her soul mate. Now she knew that whatever it was that lived in the shell of the man who she had allowed to suck the life out of her till her heart was a withered lifeless thing, wasn't capable of loving another. She couldn't understand what he gained from hurting her so much, but gaining something he definitely was. She would never understand.

Not only taking enjoyment from her hurt, but going out of his way to cause it, when she had done nothing but love and support him. Lately she'd been blaming herself for allowing him to do all that he had. Constantly finding reasons to blame herself for being stupid enough to march to his tune. Now she saw that apart from the fact that she hadn't known what he was doing, nothing in the world could justify the relentless torture over so many years purely for his sick gratification. Nothing could excuse that. No normal human being would expect such things, or even believe that another human being was capable of them. She was not to blame, and it was futile trying to understand. Long buried memories brought the shame of her desperate attempts to live and love with this man. The memories of the joy in his expression, the glee, every time she fell. When he'd mocked her. Belittled her. Scared her. Those expressions on his face that she had never allowed herself to believe she was seeing. She had seen them, because they'd been there, but she'd never believed them. How could anyone believe a smile in the face of pain.

She had thought that she could stay. Stay until she could leave without fear of homelessness and poverty, but now she realised that she couldn't stay. Finally understanding the magnitude of his disrespect. The scope and breadth of his attacks, and the size of the injury he had caused, she knew she had to leave with or without her plants. Every minute in the circle of his foul aura chipped away another piece of her soul, and she didn't think she could afford to lose any more of that. She had thought that she would be safe to stay here for just a while, but now she realised that she would be safer sleeping in a storm drain in hurricane season.

It hit her now. After her breakdown, his apparent kindness in that he backed off, and the fall down fighting stopped hadn't been because of any concern or affection. It had been because he didn't have to do anything then to terrify or upset her, because back then that was her permanent state of being. All he had to do was watch and enjoy her suffering. Her battle with what she perceived as her own madness. And on those very few occasions when he had bought something for her, or done something nice. Those times had been to make himself look good, and not because he cared for her. Even her anger made him happy. She forced herself to focus.

"What about the business?" she asked.

For just a second his eyes darkened, whether with fear or anger she couldn't tell.

"Don't you worry about that," he said, looking around the room. "I've been hoping to get help from Mr Young. I'm still not discounting that, but at this rate—. It's probably too late for that. I want to sell up quickly. Maybe sell the house with the contents."

"You've never mentioned leaving before." Irritation was quickly replacing Donna's fright.

"I've been thinking about it for a while now," he said. "The business isn't really going anywhere. I've got a bunch of lazy, stealing bums working for me anyway. In fact, there's no point in even trying to sell that. Just the house."

His phone rang. He jumped up and headed upstairs to his study, leaving her standing there, still not knowing whether or not she was included in his plans. She didn't want to be included, and knew that no matter what happened she would not be moving anywhere with Marco. He didn't know that though. He simply didn't care. She poured herself a double gin and tonic, and took it outside to her rose garden, sipping as she breathed in their heady perfume. Her plans for the following weeks couldn't happen now, but neither could she continue her life as it had been. Looking around at the splendour of life and beauty she had created in her garden, she realised that life was waiting for her to live it too. She sipped her drink and closed her eyes, the warm breeze, and the buzzing of bees further relaxing her. It was time for her to leave. With nothing if necessary. Enough was enough. She would go and speak to Elvira and the others tomorrow, and start planning her next move.

Chapter Eighteen

Marco hadn't gone to work as he always did, straight after his breakfast. He hadn't even showered or changed out of his track suit. Donna spent the morning watching him pace up and down, not taking any of the calls to his constantly ringing phone. Finally, just as she'd put his evening meal on the table, he slumped on the couch and put the television on. He hadn't missed going to work for years. She felt a twinge of pity for him when it became clear that he was in some sort of trouble. Serious trouble, and she could see he was hurting. About to offer him a cup of coffee and some sympathy, she stopped in her tracks. Her cheeks flushed with a rush of anger and shame. How could she still be so stupid after all that he had done to her?

"I have to go out," she said to the back of his head. "Elvira's expecting me to help with the ladies cheese and wine evening."

He jumped a little, but didn't turn to face her.

"Fine," he said, his voice sounding thick, as if he'd been crying.

"Your supper's on the table," she said.

"Fine."

She stood staring at his head for a while, wondering if she should be afraid. Afraid of the repercussions of whatever it was that he had done wrong. For the first time since she'd known him she felt nothing. The sympathy was gone, and she was done being frightened. Whatever it was that had got him into such a state was none of her business, and whatever happened to him because of it was his problem only. She went to her room for her folder and her handbag, walked past him without looking at him, and headed out of the door.

*

Elvira was doing readings when she arrived. Donna had been amazed at the accuracy of her predictions, but was still hesitant to ask for one. Just in case her darkest fears would be revealed. Maybe it was best not to know what the future held.

"Sit here," said Laurence, patting the space beside him on the couch. "I'm sure she won't be much longer. She only had two to see."

"How are things going?" asked Saul. "Elvira told us you're planning a big change."

Donna nodded. "I am," she said. "Marco came back early though. He's home now."

"Oh dear," said Laurence.

She laughed, and then stopped when she saw the genuine concern on his face.

"I think I'm going to be alright," she said. "I'll just have to go about things differently."

"Do you have a plan?"

She nodded. "I'm going to take Elvira up on her offer, and stay here till I'm on my feet. First though, I'm going to have try to move as many of my plants as possible here. I won't be able to ever go back for anything after I leave. That's one thing I'm absolutely sure of."

"That's the best news I've heard all day!" said Elvira, coming up behind them with a jar of freshly decanted red wine. "We can all jump in and start moving them across tomorrow."

"Marco's back," said Laurence.

"Oh dear," said Elvira.

"Also," said Donna. "He stayed home today. He never does that. He hasn't taken any calls at all, and his phone's been ringing constantly. He looks frightened too, so I'm sure he's done something bad. And he's talking about selling the house and moving out of the country. To Australia. I can't move anything out until I know what he's doing and where he will be."

"That rings alarm bells for sure. He's in trouble, and if that's the case, you need to get out faster," said Elvira. "You don't want to be in line for any fallout from his problems."

"That's right," said Laurence. "I have been wondering though. Is there any other way to get to your gardens and the old farmstead without going through the new property above it? That's quite a slope down to it, and it's highly unlikely that the original entrance would have been on the upper side of your property."

"I have no idea." The thought had never occurred to Donna, and she'd never ventured very far into the forest beyond the land she tended. As far as she knew the wilderness started there, and continued for vast distances over mountainous territory before there was any other form of civilization.

"We need to look," he said. "The front of that old house faces the forest. So do all the outbuildings, so it makes sense that the entrance would face the road in. If there is a way, then you can leave right away, and we can all jump in and move what you need moved without your husband having a clue. The most important thing now is for you to get out. You call me when you find out when he'll be out, and we can come and see what we can find."

"How exciting this all is," said Sandy, squeezing in next to Donna. "We're going to break you out of there. Don't you worry about a thing."

Elvira insisted on showing her around the house, now that she had made up her mind to come and stay. And the whole group followed, drinks in hand.

"This will be your room."

Donna walked around the huge bedroom, looking at the four poster bed and antique dresser, imagining herself in this peaceful room, finally at peace with herself. There were glass doors leading out to a small enclosed space. It was completely cobbled with a tinkling water feature in the centre, and an old wooden bench up against the wall was flanked by potted fuchsias.

"It's beautiful," she said. "Thank you Elvira." Tears of gratitude threatened, and she swallowed hard to stop them.

"No need for thanks." Elvira's eyes also glistened. "I'm looking forward to having company. Once this band of gardening gurus goes home every day, it can get a little too quiet around here."

Laurence walked her to her car again. It was a habit now, and one that she enjoyed.

"I'm glad you're getting out of there," he said. "I worry about you all alone in that house without proper security."

He took her left hand in his, looking down at her naked fingers, and shook his head.

"Call me the minute you know he'll be away, and we'll get there as fast as we can."

*

Marco was in the same spot she'd left him, his supper untouched.

"Would you like a drink?" she asked, hoping for a talk. He nodded. She poured a strong whisky and soda for him, and a glass of wine for herself, and then went to sit opposite him.

"Are you not feeling well?"

"I'm fine," he said, his grey complexion giving lie to the words. "It's just—. Some people give me such a hard time. I get so angry. They force me to lose my temper. I don't understand people sometimes. I'm only doing what I have to do. For the sake of the business. And to keep a roof over our heads."

He looked at her sullenly, with angry eyes.

"You don't realise how hard it is for me sometimes. How hard it is to keep up this life you're so used to."

His self-pitying words and tone made her nauseous again, and it took a lot of self control not to let rage take over. But she wanted to know more, so she stopped the angry things from tumbling from her mouth, wondering at the fact that she could hate anyone enough that they made her physically sick to her stomach.

"I'm sorry," she said.

The self pity on his face gave way to the slyness she knew so well, when he thought he had her fooled about one thing or another.

"The company has had to take out a couple of loans over the years," he said. "That's why I'm always trying to be frugal, but even so, there's quite a bit owing now."

Donna coughed to conceal her laughter. Marco clearly didn't understand the meaning of the word frugal, and he'd certainly never personally tried frugality in all the time she'd known him.

"Is that why you mentioned going to Australia? To start over?"

He grinned at her. "*Exactly*. I don't see why I should have to pay these bums whining at my door all the time. I'm really glad you agree with me."

His face lit up, excited now, thinking that she would do whatever she needed to do to help save him, as she always had. He leaned forward.

"What we have to do first. Tomorrow in fact. We have to transfer this house into your name. Then we sell it. Fast. They can't touch it if it's in your name. Then we take the money and go."

"How much do you—? How much does the company owe? Is there no chance of using the money from the house to pay the loans?"

"Don't be stupid Donna! If I do that I'll have nothing left to start again. Never you mind how much is owed. I don't see why I should pay it. Those guys aren't short of a buck, so it's not as if they'll go hungry or anything like that. They're bloody crooked too."

"What do you want me to do?"

"You just come along with me tomorrow, and we'll get the ball rolling. I think I might know someone who will buy this house straight away if the price is right. Although I'll check out the market first." He jumped up in his excitement. "It's another adventure Donna. It's going to be a blast. Just you wait and see."

Donna smiled and agreed, picturing her room in Elvira's house, where she'd never have to participate in any of Marco's twisted adventures ever again.

*

He was up and dressed when she came down to the kitchen, talking on his phone.

"You won't regret it Barnie," he said. "Just give me a couple of weeks. I promise. I won't let you down. You'll have every cent back."

She filled the kettle, listening to his lies.

"It worked," he said, looking fondly down at his apparent accomplice. "They won't suspect a thing, and before they know what's hit them I'll be long gone. We just have to act normal, and carry on as if we're not planning anything."

Donna just smiled, sickened to be even a small part of his dishonesty. Life was like a game to him, and he always had to win, even if winning meant tripping everyone else up. Always blaming others for his nasty actions, and feeling entitled to anything he wanted. Stealing wasn't a word that applied to him no matter what he did.

"You go get dressed. I've got an appointment with an attorney. He says that it generally takes four to six weeks to get ownership of a house transferred, and during that time I'll arrange for the sale, and start getting ready to go."

She quailed at the thought of spending hours in close proximity to him, but she had to keep up the pretence, so she dressed as fast as she could, and sat in tense silence beside him as the powerful car hurtled down the road. She was convinced now that he drove like an idiot when she was with him purely for the joy of seeing her scared. Usually she pleaded with him to slow down and at least try and keep his eyes on the road, but this time she said nothing.

They spent very little time signing the papers. Marco was jolly, talking about how he wanted to make sure his wife was secure if anything should happen to him, and berating himself for not transferring ownership to her years ago. Donna had to straighten out her sneer listening to him. The man who refused to buy life insurance for his wife and child because he believed that when he was dead, he was dead, and not responsible for looking after the living. She had a feeling that the attorney didn't quite believe him, often looking over at her with a slightly concerned frown on his face. Finally they were done, and after another hair raising drive, she was home. He stayed in the idling car.

"I'm going to take the car into the shop and get it fixed," he said. "This little bit of damage will bring the price down when I sell it. I'll overnight in town until it's ready."

"Oh." Donna was delighted at the prospect of him going away again. "How long—?"

"Couple of days," he replied, looking at her coldly. Even while he was pretending to be nice to her, he couldn't conceal his irritation at what he thought was her neediness. He didn't wait for her to reply, gunned the engine, and was gone.

With her heart singing, she rushed inside to phone Elvira and Laurence.

*

They arrived early, Elvira, Laurence, Sandy and Saul. She laughed when Saul popped an ancient pith helmet on his head and pulled a walking stick from the boot of his car. They were all dressed for hiking, and joking and laughing as always. Laurence threw an arm around her shoulders.

"Come on then," he said. "To the wilds we go."

She told them all that had transpired with Marco as they headed down the terraces.

"In a couple of weeks you're going to own this whole property," said Sandy. "Once you do, apply for a divorce and boot the bastard out. The prenup he insisted on will bite him in the bum then, and there won't be a thing he can do about it."

"I couldn't do that."

"Why ever not?" Elvira asked. "After all that he's done to you, he deserves to face the music for whatever it is that he's done. And you don't deserve to leave with nothing after all the years you've put up with his malice."

"It's not worth it," said Laurence. "If my mother had pulled a stunt like that, my father would have killed her."

"You're right," said Saul. "Crazy's still crazy no matter how well it's hidden, and you never know what this guy is capable of when he's cornered."

Elvira and Sandy finally agreed.

"It's just a house after all," said Elvira. "Still. You've put your heart into this place all of these years, and it's a shame that you have to walk away with nothing to show for it."

Donna's heart constricted. She did love this place, and she knew that she would miss it when she was gone. Especially the old farmstead, and her secret gardens.

"You're right Laurie." Elvira stopped at the farmhouse porch. "Sometimes one chance is all you get, and with the state he's already in the most important thing is to get Donna well away from him."

They stood on the top step and looked around. Over the decades the forest wildflowers and grasses had filled up every nook and cranny, so the old driveway wasn't visible, if it was there at all.

"Logic," said Saul. "We have to look at the tree growth. Find the youngest and smallest and then we'll know where to go.

"Right," said Sandy, linking arms with him, and following Elvira into the forest. "Put your psychic hat on Elvira."

"I do actually have a strong feeling that we should simply move in a straight line," she said.

"There's a wide stream behind the clearing," said Donna. "So it probably won't be to the right unless there's a bridge somewhere."

"Straight ahead people," said Elvira. "Straight ahead."

They advanced slowly, not so much delayed by the long grasses, but rather by one or another of them stopping to examine some beauty of the plant world. Spring had brought some stunning wildflower displays. It soon became obvious that they were walking through two distinct rows of Maple trees, and finally, after a sharp turn to the left between a pair of towering trees, they came to the road. Donna looked around, and calculated that this point must be quite a distance from their usual entrance.

"Easy," said Saul. "We can leave the grass as it is close to the road, so as not to attract the wrong kind of attention, and we can clear the rest in a couple of days. Just as well there's such an angle through the trees coming in here. If you don't know where to look you would never realise there's an entrance here. Maybe the original owners also grew illegal pot plants."

"There you go," said Laurence. "We have a secret entrance to your secret garden."

Donna smiled, enjoying his proximity. Being physically close to him had the opposite effect that being close to Marco had. She felt warm and safe. She knew he liked her. She knew that all of her new friends liked her just the way she was, but she found it a little strange. The fact that they knew her secrets now, the secret of her pathetic life, and still chose to help and support her made her want to weep with gratitude. There was always the underlying fear that they would abandon her. Laugh at her and call her stupid. Tell her that they'd just being having a little fun, and that Marco was right. That she was worthless.

Not concentrating on where she was walking, she stumbled over a hidden rock, and time slowed as she realised that there was no way she could stop her fall. But he caught her. She felt his strong arm quickly encircle her waist and pull her up against him. She hadn't been this close to another human being for a very long time. Even Shelley avoided physical contact. Now with her face pressed against his chest, she inhaled the smell of him, and delighted in the feel of him.

"Are you alright?"

Suddenly feeling like a thief. A stealer of physical contact, she pushed herself away, knowing that the heat rising in her face meant that she was blushing the blush that Marco always said emphasised her freckles – in a bad way. She looked around and realised that they were alone. She was grateful that they had fallen behind and the others hadn't witnessed her pathetic stumble.

"Fine. I'm fine. Thank you. Sorry—."

Finally she looked up into his face. Smiling, he moved a lock of her wild hair from her eye.

"You're beautiful," he said. "Especially when you're all pink in the face."

She didn't know what to say, so she shook her head and started back towards the farmstead, making sure to keep her eyes on the ground. Laurence walked beside her silently for the rest of the way. Her mind was racing. How stupid she was. Allowing his mere touch to affect her the way it had. How pathetic she was. Eagerly clamping on to him like some desperate school girl. She didn't have time for such nonsense now. She needed to get a grip on herself, focus on her goals, and stay as far away from Laurence Newman as possible from now on.

Chapter Nineteen

The weeks leading up to the final transfer of the property into her name had been incredibly busy for Donna. Keeping up the pretence of being the usual supportive fool that Marco still believed that she was had been the most difficult exercise in self control. Maintaining the appearance of going about her daily life as she always had done had been equally exhausting. Her friends had cleared the drive to the farmstead and made countless trips to move thousands of plants and seedlings to Elvira's nursery, but she had managed very well to keep Laurence at a distance. He'd noticed and was obviously hurt.

Each day she got stronger, and as her resolve to make a new life for herself on her own cemented, she knew that any relationship other than friendship could never take place in her life again. It hurt her deeply to know that she was hurting him, but in the long run it would be better for both of them. She couldn't understand what he saw in her. Daily as she danced to Marco's sick tune with a sharp awareness of everything he was doing, she couldn't stop the disgust at herself for being blind to his manipulations for so long, and for allowing him to mutilate her psyche so badly, to the point where she honestly couldn't remember much of most of her life with him now without a huge amount of effort. But she was making that effort. She knew that getting away from him meant that she had to remember every little hurt and twist that she could.

And now the house legally belonged to her, and Marco was trying to find a buyer. It wasn't as easy as he'd thought it would be though. The property was huge, and the house beautiful, but it was too remote for most people to want to live in, and the long commute to Wilson Springs was off-putting. That was why they'd bought it so cheaply in the first place. She could see the panic growing in him daily as he scrabbled to keep those he owed so much money to at bay. His constant griping and frantic pacing seriously disturbed her equilibrium, and she tried to work faster getting her plants packed up and moved. She was mainly moving small plants and seedlings, and working in her gardens made her sad now, knowing that she'd have to leave so many behind and that some would have to be destroyed. She was dreading the day that she'd have to get rid of all evidence of the illegal plants in her collection. They'd been incredibly difficult to get, and in the years of nurturing them she'd grown to love every one of them. They'd been her only friends. They'd been the only witnesses of her tears, fears, and sadness over the years, as she'd unconsciously tried to hold on to her sanity by investing her love in them.

Marco hired a trailer, and had her box up the antiques and treasures that she had collected during her few years of gainful employment, and a few that were the only mementoes she still had of her forgotten family. She did as he told her, ignoring the twinges of regret as she packed her possessions away, never to be seen again.

"Amazing how much crap you've collected," he said, loading the last of the boxes. "Still. This lot should make a good couple of bucks."

"Yes," she said.

He grinned, peering into her eyes. "This upsets you," he said.

She shook her head. "No it doesn't. They're just things. Things aren't important to me these days."

The smile disappeared from his face, and she knew that he would think up something that really would upset her now. She tried to remember how she would have felt in this situation six months ago. She would have been devastated. Terrified. The way he liked her to be. Now she just wanted to never have to see his face ever again.

"I shouldn't be more than a couple of days," he said. "I'm going to offload this lot, and then I'm going to drop the price of the house by ten grand. I want to be gone in two weeks time. I have to be gone by then."

Donna smiled at him. He still didn't talk about them going together, and the truth was that she still was unsure whether he was planning on taking her with him or not. What a crappy man he was. No. Not a man. Marco was most certainly not a man.

"Good luck," she said.

He scowled, vaguely suspicious, and turned to get into his car.

"Yeah," he said, and left.

*

One of his cell phones was on the kitchen table. She stood staring down at it, unable to touch it. He never ever left any of his phones lying around. She wasn't sure how many he had, and had originally not understood why he needed more than one. Finally she'd figured out that he had many personas as well as many lovers, and then it made sense. It started ringing as she looked down at it, and she jumped, startled. She hastily turned and headed out, planning on putting a good few hours of work packing up more plants, because she wanted to spend the following day at the old age home.

She never realised that he was there until it was too late to sneak away. He was standing looking down at the thriving cannabis plants.

"I see you," he said.

She pushed her way through the thick vegetation that obscured the clearing.

"Hi Laurence," she said.

"These guys are doing amazingly well," he said. "In all my years of gardening I've never met anyone else with such a passion for the illegal and the strange. I've just loaded your carnivorous plants. That nepenthes is a creepy little fellow. I don't even want to know how you keep them fed."

"They are a little creepy," she said, laughing, avoiding his gaze by staring at the plants instead. "So far they've kept themselves fed. It's surreal sometimes being alone with them. As if they're watching you, and wouldn't hesitate to eat you if they were a little bigger, and you were a little closer."

"How have you been?" he asked softly. "You've been avoiding me. Have I done something to upset you?"

About to mutter some feeble excuse, she hesitated. She didn't want lies to be part of her life anymore. There'd been too many of those.

"I'm sorry," she said. "You couldn't ever upset me. It's just—. I just need to sort my life out. And it's hard. I don't think I have anything more to give. And you—."

"Me what?"

"I don't want to like you too much. It's all just wrong."

He turned her around to face him, tilting her chin up so that she couldn't avoid looking into his eyes.

"I understand Donna. I know that you have to start a whole new life. And I know pretty much the sort of life you've lived till now. I also know your loyalty to Marco as your husband even though he's never been a husband to you. I wouldn't dream of trying to push you into doing anything that you don't want to do. I never want you to fear me in any way. But there's something between us. You can't deny that. I think about you all the time. Ever since the first time I met you, and you crapped on me for asking you out, I see your face every day. But I know better than to expect anything other than friendship right now. So please. Can we just be friends?"

"Can we?" she asked.

"Of course we can. I've missed you so much these past days. Whatever you want. Just please stop shutting me out and avoiding me."

Finally she smiled and nodded. He had no idea that apart from being more attracted to him than she'd ever been to any other man, the way he always treated her with kindness and respect, the way he offered his strength to hold her up, and the knowledge that if she ever needed him for anything, he would be there for her, made her anger at herself for having lived the life she'd led with Marco even worse. He might understand men like her husband better than most normal people, but nobody who hadn't actually been through life with such an evil creature could conceive of the feelings she dealt with. She wanted Laurence, but she needed her freedom and independence. She needed to know that she could look after herself.

She told him about Marco taking all her treasures to sell for bottom dollar at the antique shop, and about dropping the price of the house for a quick sale.

"He says that he wants to be gone in two weeks."

"What treasures is he selling?"

She looked at him, surprised that he'd asked. She cared less about most of them going than she'd expected to, but the anger was etched in his face.

"Mainly paintings and porcelain. Things I used to collect before I married. I don't mind too much. I tried to hold on to a couple of my Dresden figurines, but failed. I don't even think that they were worth much money, but they were the only things I managed to hold on to from my family. They were the only things my mother never sold, no matter how broke she was, because she got them from her granny. Still. Doesn't matter. Really."

"The ones on the dresser in the kitchen?"

"Yes," she said, unable to prevent a smile. Laurence noticed everything.

"What an asshole that man is," he said. "Are you coming to Elvira's later?"

She confirmed that she was, walked him to the truck, and then wandered back to the farmhouse. She looked around the old kitchen fondly. She'd had some wonderful times in this house. The previous owners had left a few pieces of old furniture, including a beautiful yellowwood table, surrounded by mismatched antique chairs. She sat down and opened her notebook, checking her list to see what still needed to be done before she could leave. They would harvest the final batch of cannabis, and find somewhere safe to store it. That would last a good while before they'd have to pay for it again, because there definitely wasn't going to be any more planted.

She couldn't concentrate very well today. Her mind kept wandering to Laurence. It occurred to her that rather than getting in the way of her inner healing, his affection for her had been giving her more strength. There was something about someone liking you. Wanting your company. It definitely had started her respecting herself a little more. These past days filled with tiring physical activity, and playing mental games with Marco hadn't left much time or energy for thoughts of anything else. She walked slowly back to the main house, planning only a long bath before she drove to Elvira's. She jumped, startled to see Shelley sitting at the kitchen table, scowling at Marco's cell phone in her hand.

Donna rushed over and kissed her daughter's forehead.

"Goodness!" she said. "What a lovely surprise."

Shelley was clearly furious about something. "What the hell's going on Mom? I've been trying to phone you for weeks."

Donna fished her phone out of her pocket, looking at it in confusion. "I haven't got any calls from you."

"Hand it over."

She passed the phone to Shelley, who briskly clicked away at it. She was a genius with technology.

"You've blocked my number," she said. "Here. Look."

Donna took her phone back, completely at a loss as to what had happened.

"I didn't. I wouldn't do that my love. You must know that."

"It's not something you can do by accident Mom. Someone physically has to do it. And if you didn't then who did? And why? And what's up with Dad? I had some weirdo phone me last week looking

185

for him. Ugh. He kept saying that he was going to cut his balls off if he didn't call him back. Then last night another call from Dad himself asking me to loan him ten thousand dollars. What the hell? You guys are loaded." She pointed to Marco's phone. "And there's some seriously weird things on that too."

"Marco. Marco must have blocked your number on my phone."

But why? Donna lowered herself into a chair, trying to assimilate all Shelley had just said. The thought that anyone connected to Marco's filthy private life had access to her child made her blood run cold. She'd never wanted her to find out what her father truly was, and had never had any intention of ever telling her, but now she realised that there was no choice. Marco wouldn't care at all for her safety, and the fact that he'd contacted her for money meant that he must be desperate. The foul mouthed caller could only have got her number from Marco. She couldn't leave her in the dark anymore. She picked up her phone to call Elvira and let her know that she wouldn't be coming through tonight.

"Grab a bottle of wine and a couple of glasses my love," she said. "It's going to be a long night."

Her daughter was a lot less surprised to hear what she had to say than she'd thought she would be. She was also amazed at the courage and strength that her child possessed. Shelley went through the messages on her father's phone, reading them out loud to Donna, and together they pieced together a little of what his problems were. It was obvious that Marco was buying cocaine for Jackie and himself, and had been for a very long time. Judging by her frantic, pleading messages, he'd dumped her. There were several messages from people who appeared to be really angry loan sharks, and few hundred missed calls from his company and his bankers. And several chilling threats from someone who could only be a drug dealer.

"I'm amazed that he left it lying around like this." Shelley tossed the phone onto the table.

"He knows I would never touch it. I don't touch any of his private things."

Shelley frowned. "I'm sorry Mom," she said. "I never knew how bad things were for you."

"I never wanted anyone to know, especially you."

"I always found it strange that my own father disliked me," said Shelley. "To be honest, I've never liked him either. I knew he was tight with money, and made you go without things, but I thought you were alright that way. I thought you were happy with your life. I'm glad you're getting out now though. You could always come and stay with me you know. You should have told me before."

"I'm the one who's supposed to be looking after you though," said Donna. "I'm supposed to be strong for you. The mother. Now I'm hoping to get a business started locally, with the plants, but thank you for the offer my love."

"So what are we going to do about Dad?"

"Nothing," said Donna, getting up to find something for their supper. "He'll sell this property for some ridiculously low amount of money, and then he'll run away and never look back. I'll be out of here in a couple of days. What we do need to do is to report the person who phoned you. If he's a drug dealer or a loan shark, he could be dangerous."

Shelley looked wistfully around the kitchen. "I always loved this room," she said. "You were always making or baking something for me when I was home. It was good when Dad was away. Not when he was around and you were having screaming fights. That's when I wished I could be transported straight back to boarding school."

Donna put frozen lasagne into the microwave, wanting to apologise to her daughter for her crappy childhood. To tell her that she'd cried herself to sleep for months when she'd first taken her to boarding school. But Donna knew now that boarding school was what had saved her Shelley from a much worse childhood if she'd been home permanently in the sights of her father.

They ate their food, drank a little more wine, and spoke freely for the first time in their lives. When Donna went to bed, leaving Shelley reading her books on narcissism, she felt invigorated and ready to face the future. Her fear had disappeared in the face of a threat to her daughter. She knew what lengths Marco would go to, to save his own skin, and there was no way on Earth that she would allow him hurt her child any more than he already had. No. She was done playing games.

Chapter Twenty

Shelley had too much work waiting for her to stay any longer, and after a large breakfast she prepared to leave.

"Promise me you'll be careful," Donna passed a small basket of pickles and preserves through the car window.

"I will," said Shelley, then grinned suddenly. "I forgot to tell you. I don't live on my own anymore. Tidge moved in a month ago. Not much can hurt me with him around."

Surprise gave way to relief. Donna had met Tidge when Shelley had been sick, and Marco hadn't been able to stop her from going to spend a few days with her daughter. He was a huge bear of a man with a heart of gold, and his adoration of Shelley had been very plain to see. He was also a police detective. He wouldn't let anyone hurt her. She exhaled, thankful also that she hadn't shared the exact specifics of the plants she'd been growing when all the truth had been revealed last night.

"That is wonderful darling," she said. "Make sure that he knows everything. So. You two are serious now? Any chance of wedding bells soon?"

Shelley blushed, putting her car in gear. "You never know," she said. "Take care of yourself Mom, and phone me every day. If you don't I'll know that something's wrong."

"I will. I love you baby."

"Love you Mom."

Donna got ready to go to the old age home, and took Marco's cell phone with her. She fully intended to answer every call that came in. By the time she'd weeded and pruned several little gardens, and arrived at Elvira's shop, she knew quite a lot about the trouble her husband was in. His company was in its death throes. He owed a lot more money than the house was worth to various banks, loan sharks, and a few people who he'd tricked into believing that they were buying a share in a very healthy business. His staff hadn't been paid, and neither had his suppliers. It wouldn't be long, and he would either be legally arrested or punished in the way that loan sharks and drug dealers do. There was no way that she could see to fix the messes he had made. Marco's back was up against a wall, and he had nothing left to lose. She couldn't imagine what she'd be going through if she hadn't met Elvira.

The last call she'd taken had been from Jackie. After only a moment's hesitation she'd answered. The woman was distraught, talking to Donna, expecting sympathy, and totally overlooking the fact that she was talking to the wife of the man she was raging about. Finally she revealed that she was pregnant. Seven months pregnant with Marco's child. *Seven months.* Donna disconnected then, throwing the phone to the floor of the car, not wanting to believe what she'd just heard. She parked and then sat a while with her eyes tightly shut. There was nothing more he could do to her, but what he had done was unbelievable. She felt dirty again. Disgusted at both him for being such a devil, and for herself for allowing him to. Small and useless, that she was valued so little by her husband. She knew that his big plan to leave the country didn't include her. He would take the money from the sale of the house and leave her homeless without a second thought. Still feeling shaky, she headed in to the coffee shop, and told her friends her latest news.

"Wow man," said Saul. "No depths that asshole won't plumb."

Her friends were livid, but none more so than Laurence.

"He's pissed off some very dangerous people," he said. "And he's left you vulnerable and directly in the line of fire. They don't know that he's a psycho who doesn't give a damn about you or anyone else, and they might just think that hurting you will get them their money. No. You're getting out of there straight away now. We can collect the rest of the plants without anyone knowing, and we'll all go and pack up the rest that you want moved across. There can't be much more to do apart from harvesting the marijuana plants."

Before she could say anything her phone rang. "It's Marco," she said, letting it ring.

They all stared at it until it stopped, and then it started again.

"Hello," she said, unafraid, feeling the eyes of people who cared about her on her.

"What the hell are you doing?" he shouted. "Why don't you answer your damn phone?"

"I—."

"Just listen to me," he said. "I've found a cash buyer for the house. He'll be coming around tomorrow afternoon. I've sold the Bentley but I've got a rental, so I'll be home tomorrow around noon. Then I have a bit of business to do, so it'll just be a flying visit."

"Oh," she said.

"See you tomorrow," he said, and disconnected.

Donna looked around at her friend's shocked faces and burst out laughing.

"There is no way I can get the cannabis out of there by tomorrow afternoon, and whoever the buyer is, is going to want to see all of what he's buying."

After much frantic discussion it was decided that they would all head out to the farmstead immediately, and burn what they couldn't move out. Donna felt both terror and excitement looking in her rear view mirror at the following headlights. She could hardly believe the way her life had turned out, but she was deeply grateful for the people now in it. They wouldn't leave her in trouble.

They loaded as much of the illegal plants and cannabis as they could, wanting to save it for the old people, but finally as the sun peeped over the horizon they could do no more.

"Time for a little fire," said Saul.

The stench of the burning drug was sickening, and Donna was terrified that some passerby would smell it. She lifted the top of her shirt to cover her face. Laurence came over and put his arm around her waist.

"Stinks, doesn't it?" he said. "Shame we have to lose so much."

"There's plenty money to buy it for the old folk," said Elvira. "I must say though, that I loved watching it grow."

"Me too," said Sandy. "It's a pity that people are so greedy and twisted. If it was treated with the respect it deserves it would stop a great deal of pain."

"I kind of liked being a big time criminal for a while," said Saul. "You'd do proper time for growing the amount of weed that we have."

Laurence's grip tightened, and she looked up at him.

"What now?" he asked.

"I'll go and get cleaned up and wait," she said. "Once Marco gets whatever money he's getting for the house, he'll just leave, I'm sure."

Laurence nodded, unable to keep the concern from his face.

"I'm finding it really hard to leave you like this."

"I'll be fine," she said, hoping that would be true.

They hosed down the final flames, and upended a trailer of manure over the evidence.

"There," said Sandy. "You're safe now."

Laurence grunted. "Put me on speed dial Donna, and keep your phone in your hand all the time till this is over. Do it now."

She did as he said, although she was sure that there wouldn't be any drama this time. Marco wanted money, and he wanted to run away. He would be all charm till he got what he wanted. Still, it felt really good to know how much Laurence cared.

"You go on home," said Saul. "We'll finish up here. Try and get some sleep."

"Thank you so much," said Donna, looking around at them with tears in her eyes. "I'm so grateful—."

"Hush," said Elvira, coming over and giving her a hug. "You just get through this day safely, and we'll all be here waiting to celebrate your new life."

After getting hugged by all of them, she went over to her car, and headed out on to the road and home. It felt odd pulling in to the drive, looking at the house that had been her home for over thirty years. Walking down the passage, looking at occasional tables bare of the things that she had once proudly dusted once a week, and the telltale squares of absent paintings on the walls did bring regret. Not so much regret of the loss of them, as much as regret of the loss of the years of her life when she had thought wrongly that she had a home. She'd never had a home with Marco. She headed for the shower, utterly exhausted.

Chapter Twenty One

As Donna waited for Marco her anxiety levels had soared. She wondered if he was expecting her to do anything, so she paced the house, picking things up and wondering if she should pack them in boxes. She reversed her car out of the garage and opened the boot to start packing as many of her things that she could squeeze in. It was still stuffed full of the cannabis they'd harvested the previous night, so she wouldn't get much in there. There were also a few canisters of opium poppy seeds. She shut it, and checked her watch, wondering if there was time to drive down the road and offload it somewhere before he arrived. He arrived just as she got to the kitchen and grabbed her phone. He walked through the door, looking cool as a cucumber in his tailored suit, the scent of his Clive Christian cologne wafting around him. She grunted. Maybe if he'd spent a little less on things like that, he wouldn't be on the run now.

"Ready for action?" he asked.

Donna slid her phone into her pocket and sat down. She was way too tired and stressed to pretend she knew what he meant.

"Marco," she said. "I have no idea what's actually supposed to happen here. What exactly is it that you want me to do? And what's going to happen? Once the house is sold."

He moved quickly to the table, sitting down opposite her and leaning forward, smiling warmly. He covered her hands with his own, and for a second the memory of him doing exactly that on the night he'd proposed made her dizzy.

"My darling. My Bella Donna," he said softly. "I'm so sorry for all the running up and down lately. All the confusion. I've been so stressed. Trust me my darling. Everything will work out just fine."

She looked into his eyes, seeing the dancing joy there. Marco loved drama. Good or bad. Using his old pet name for her, one that he'd stopped using a year into their marriage, not only cut her like a knife, but made her realise that he really needed her now. That she was key to him succeeding in his plan. She smiled back at him, nodded, and gently removed her hands from beneath his.

"Yes," she said. "But what exactly is it that's going to happen?"

"I've found the perfect buyer for the house. Its rural location, and the fact that in all the years I've lived here I've never once seen a cop around, or many other people either, means that it will be perfect for his business. What people get up to after I'm gone isn't my business. He's bringing cash notes. I've got all the paperwork in my briefcase. All you have to do is sign, we get the money, the end."

"And then when will we have to leave the house? Will there be time to pack a few things. All my kitchen things—."

Marco threw back his head and laughed.

"What're you worried about such silly things for? No. He's buying it as is. All included except for personal things. We need to be out in three days, but that will be fine. Once I've got the cash today, I'll go straight out and sort everything we need, and then while I'm gone you can get your clothes and so on ready to go, and I'll call you with the hotel details."

The last thing in the world Donna wanted to do was go anywhere with Marco now, but he didn't know that, and logically there was no reason for her not to go with him right now if he was being genuine with her.

"Can't I come with you today?" she asked. "This is all very frightening."

He leaned back, looking at her through slitted eyes. She could see that regardless of the trouble he was in, he was truly enjoying watching her go through this. A part of her wanted to hurt him back. Wanted to see him crash and burn. All the years she'd been with him, she'd always been loyal in every way, no matter what he did. But even though that angered her, she realised that that was just who she was. She didn't have it in her to purposely hurt anyone. Not even Marco. Not even now.

"Don't be silly," he said. "I have business to wrap up. You need to get ready. I'll call you when I'm done."

"What about Shelley?"

"What about Shelley?" he sneered. "She's a big girl, with her own business. She hardly ever visits you anyway. She's not going to care whether you live in this house or not."

Donna couldn't look at him now, knowing that he would certainly see the fury in her eyes. He was the only reason their daughter stayed away. Her hatred of him made her feel sick. She quickly pushed her chair back, and started out the door.

"There's no time for smelling roses now," he called after her. "How about a coffee?"

She kept walking, needing the serenity that her garden always brought. She heard a car horn. The buyer must have arrived. She leaned over and plucked a pale pink freesia flower, holding under her nostrils and breathing in deeply.

"Donna," shouted Marco from the doorway. "Our guest is here."

She looked down at the beautiful bloom in her hand. She didn't often cut flowers unless she was preparing a medication. She preferred to see them living under the sun, not dying in a vase. Sorry that she'd picked this one, she dropped it to the ground, regretting that she had shortened its life. Then she forced a smile and went into the house.

Darryl Hart looked like a B grade movie pimp, and sounded like one too, but was clearly not short of money. Wearing a shiny white suit, most of his fingers sported several gold rings. He was possibly the burliest short man she had ever met. She took the hand he held out and almost yelped when he clamped down hard. His face told the stories of fights with knives.

"Well now Marco," he said. "Such a pretty little woman you've been hiding out here in the sticks."

"Yes," said Marco. "And she makes great coffee too."

Donna put the machine on and prepared a tray for their drinks, darting glances at the two men chatting and laughing at the table. Marco looked in the briefcase packed tightly with wads of cash that Darryl put in front of him.

"I won't bother counting it," he said. "I know I can trust you." He closed the briefcase and put it on the floor under the table, then went out to get his own briefcase.

Donna brought the coffee tray over.

"Would you like to look around?" she asked.

Darryl shook his head. "Nah," he said. "I'm more interested in the location than the decor." The smile that had started disappeared. He leaped from his chair, and with snakelike speed pulled a pistol from inside his jacket.

Donna followed his gaze. Marco had returned. But not alone. Behind him was a man pressing a gun tightly to his jaw. Another suited man walked in behind them.

"Put that thing away Darryl," he said. "You could hurt yourself with that."

"What the hell are you doing here?" Darryl kept his weapon pointed straight at the man's face.

"I was about to ask you the same question." The man walked straight over to Donna, grasped her chin tightly, and lifted her face up. "Hello there pretty lady," he said. "What's your name?"

Donna had no choice but to stand up, as the strong hand gripping her face pulled. She'd never been so frightened.

"Donna," she said.

"Ah," he said. "The lovely Mrs McGee. You can call me Doc."

She nodded, relieved when he let go of her chin. She stood where she was, too terrified to move.

"How very fortuitous finding you here Darryl," said Doc. "Killing two birds with one stone if you like. So let us get straight to the point. You gentlemen owe me a substantial amount of money. Also you've been avoiding me. Now that's just rude. My feelings are hurt."

"You'll get it all," whimpered Marco. "I promise. I'm expecting a huge payout in two days."

"Really?" asked Doc. "The same payout you were expecting a month ago? No. You've had enough chances. And what have you got to say Darryl? You take my cash and you don't deliver. I've been waiting two weeks now. What kind of service is that?"

Doc nodded at the man holding the gun to Marco's neck, and the subtle movement of his hand made Donna realise that this was real, and she was probably going to die along with her crooked husband. These people were clearly not talking about your average business transaction, and she could see that they weren't holding weapons that they weren't prepared to use. The metallic click of a revolver being cocked was all she needed to hear. Without allowing herself to think any further, she bolted for her car. She made it to the driveway before she was tackled to the ground. A heavy arm pressed down on her neck, painfully pushing her cheek into the gravel. She closed her eyes tightly, waiting for the bullet.

Then there was running, men shouting, gunshots, and a car engine revving and roaring away. The pressure on her was lifted, and then more car engines. Donna remained motionless for some time before opening her eyes and looking around. The only vehicle remaining in the drive was Marco's rental. She quailed, remembering that she had left her keys in the ignition. And the boot was filled with several kilograms of freshly harvested marijuana and enough opium seeds to get her arrested for a very long time. She shot up and called Laurence. She could hear his running feet before she was disconnected.

He phoned her back a half an hour later.

"There's been an accident. Not far from the farmstead drive. Your car and two others," he said. "Three guys are dead, but your husband seems alright."

"I'm coming," she said, running out to the rental car. "Don't call the police or anyone yet. Wait. The cannabis is still in the boot of my car. Can you take it out?"

"Oh shit," he said. "Don't worry. I'll sort it out. Another car's just pulled up. Just don't worry. It will be alright."

Donna drove faster than she ever had in her life. She was going to jail. After all was done, Marco had won. Because of his dishonesty and cowardice, she knew that there was no way out of this. Idiot! She slowed when she arrived at the scene of the crash, horrified at the sight. She saw Laurence's vehicle and one other, thankful that there were no police yet.

"Mom!"

Donna stopped in her tracks. Her daughter ran to her and threw her arms around her, sobbing.

"Shelley?"

"Oh Mom. I thought it was you. When I saw your car—."

Much as she wanted to comfort her child, Donna knew that speed was imperative. She looked at Tidge leaning over Marco, and Laurence standing beside him. He looked at her and very distinctly put his forefinger over his lips. He wanted her to keep quiet. And then with a shock that sent cold tremors through her body, she saw the open boot of her car.

"Come my love." She rubbed Shelley's back and kissed her forehead, then took her hand and pulled her over to Marco.

Tidge's expression was all cop on the job. Marco got to his feet, and glared at her.

"What the fuck?" he shouted. "What the fuck is a shitload of pot and drugs doing in the boot of your car?"

"Shut up!" yelled Shelley. "Mom would *never* be involved with drugs. *It's you.*" She turned to Tidge. "It's him. He's never cared about us. And wherever he was going with that stuff in the boot has got *nothing* to do with my mother. I told you about the drug dealer on his phone."

Tidge nodded. "Anything to say Donna?"

Before Donna could respond, Marco carried on shouting. Only now he was screeching at his daughter.

"You shut up, you little bitch. You have no idea—."

He got no further. After the tiniest expression of disgust flitted across his features, Tidge moved fast, and holding Marco up by the front of his shirt with one hand, he pushed his badge into his face with the other.

"You have the right to remain silent," he began.

Marco paled, pushing Tidge's hand away from him. He looked around, eyes flickering briefly over Laurence, and then behind Donna, where the rental vehicle stood idling. Then he ran for it even though it was obvious that he would never make it. Tidge started after him.

"No!"

Donna didn't want anyone arrested for what she was guilty of. Tidge stopped, and looked back at her. Marco threw himself into the car, wove it crazily between the debris, and sped down the road towards

Wilson Springs. Laurence rushed to her and held her tightly to his chest. When she looked up again, she saw Tidge forcing down the boot of her car.

"I don't know what's going on here," he said. "And this goes against everything I believe in, but for now we'll tow your vehicle back home. If we don't, you're going to be in a world of trouble no matter whose drugs those are."

He nodded in the direction of the two smashed cars.

"I recognise them. One of the deceased is Doc Simon Nixon. Drug lord. And another is Darryl Hart. Supplier of anything from drugs, to stolen goods and stolen people. It's not a coincidence that these three vehicles piled up in the same heap. I'm doing this for Shelley. And because I believe that she believes you have nothing to do with what was going down here."

He walked over to them, and held out his hand to Laurence.

"You two are obviously already acquainted," he said. "I'm Tidge."

After introductions, Laurence helped hook Donna's car to Tidge's, and they left the scene. Once Donna's car was safely locked away in the garage, Tidge phoned and reported the accident to the local police without revealing that he was an officer of the law.

Donna discreetly put the briefcase full of cash in the cupboard under the sink, and wondered what Marco would do now. He'd been about to be arrested, and he'd run away from the policeman doing the arresting. He'd never met Tidge before, but he wasn't stupid, and he must realise that his daughter was involved with him in some way, so it was unlikely that he would come back here any time soon.

Shelley explained their surprise visit, holding out her hand to show off her tanzanite engagement ring. Donna hugged them both.

"I'm so happy," she said. "Welcome to the family Tidge."

The four of them sat out on the patio, sipping champagne.

"Did you know about your husband's dealing with drugs Donna?" asked Tidge.

She could truthfully answer that she hadn't, still feeling bad that the cannabis she'd grown was considered her husband's. If anyone checked for fingerprints on the packages it would quickly become apparent that they weren't.

"What happened to your face?"

Donna flushed, remembering the pain and terror when she'd been held down by that thug. Anger squashed the guilt. Marco. Selfish to the end. He hadn't cared that she was being hurt. He just jumped in her car and drove away, knowing that he was leaving her with killers. She squared her jaw, and prepared to save herself.

"Marco was having a meeting with those three gentlemen outside in the driveway. I don't know what happened. I heard yelling and gunshots, and then I heard the cars speed out. I ran outside and tripped. I panicked, not knowing what to do, and then after a while I decided to drive to town because Marco wasn't answering his phone. I thought—. And then I found you two, with him. At the accident."

Tidge looked at her for such a long time, that she was beginning to squirm. She knew he wanted to ask her why the drugs had been in her car, but he didn't.

"You don't seem overly surprised by the events of today," he said to Laurence.

"I'm not," said Laurence. "Donna's husband is not a very nice man."

"What do you think about the evidence in the boot?"

"It has nothing to do with Donna," replied Laurence. "Myself and all the rest of her friends will swear to that. And if the fact that it is in her car can hurt her in any way. Well then. It would be better if it weren't."

"Right then," said Tidge, getting up. "I suggest a little bonfire Donna. Where could we do that?"

They burned the cannabis and canisters of opium behind her shed. Relieved as she was to see it go up in flames, she did feel a twinge of regret at the loss of the medicine.

Tidge turned and smiled at Donna. She could see that he knew she hadn't been telling the whole truth.

"So, soon to be mother in law," he said. "That is that."

*

She stayed with Laurence on the patio after Shelley and Tidge went up to bed.

"What do you think he'll do?" he asked.

"Anything's possible with Marco," she said, and quietly told him what really had happened that afternoon.

"I'm commandeering your couch tonight," he said angrily. "I'm not leaving you until we know for sure what he's up to."

She nodded. "I'd like that," she said.

"How are you feeling?" he asked. "You've had a terrible day."

"I'm alright," she said, knowing that it was true. "I'm going to be alright."

"The way he spoke to you and your daughter," he said. "It was hard not to step up and punch him. Tidge didn't mess around though. Nice guy."

"He doesn't usually swear like that," she said. "He's subtle with his barbs. With Shelley he likes to talk about my parents. Her bloodline. Telling her what pathetic losers they were, and that she takes after them. Insulting her talents and calling her business a cop out from real life. Me. Everything's fair game."

"I'm sorry," he said. "Nobody deserves that. My father used to call my mom a dago. Among other things. He used to use words like that to their friends too. Although they accepted them as jokes. I always used to wonder why they couldn't see that he meant what he said. They all thought my mother was horrible to him. He cultivated that. She was so dissociated from reality, I think she believed it too. Believed that she was the problem."

"Marco too," she said. "All of his friends think I'm an unstable, stuck up, frigid loser. They feel sorry for him. For supporting me. He makes sure that that's what everyone sees. People would never believe what he's really done. I didn't even know until recently. His fakery to cover the fact that he truly has no real humanity is a fine art. He takes on the mannerisms of other people when he feels that he should be showing empathy or emotion. I still find it hard to believe anyone could be as stupid as I have. I let him unhinge me, not knowing that he was the one who was sick all along. Meeting Elvira, and all of you is what saved me. All of you believing me. Wanting tomatoes saved me."

He smiled. "We've all had our share of bad situations. Not to the scale that you have though. Finding out about this narcissistic mental illness from you, and also from what I've been looking up myself is a totally shocking learning curve. It's like someone was living in my house and writing down all the things my father did. I can't imagine what you must be going through now, and I'm sure that you have a way to go to recover completely, but I want you to know that I will be there for you every step of the way. Mentally and physically. I mean physically in the way that Marco will never invade your space again if you don't want him to."

Donna blinked. Unaccustomed feelings overwhelming her for a moment. Looking at Laurence now, she remembered the first months with Marco. Months where she'd felt safe, believing that he would always be there for her. There to protect and love her forever. Laurence made her feel that way now. Safe and cared for. She wondered if he was capable of being like her husband, and waiting until he had her isolated and vulnerable, and then grinding her down with almost every imaginable abusive psychological tactic.

They both stared down at her phone when it began to ring. Marco. She answered on speaker and left it on the table between them.

"I have no idea what the fuck you were doing with a boot load of pot you bitch," he screeched. "But pinning it on *me*. If you think you're going to get away with it you're seriously mistaken. Nobody—."

Laurence hit the disconnect button.

"Listen," said Marco when he phoned again. "I'm sorry. I'm all wound up. Listen. I need you to bring me the money. Where's that cop?"

"Where do you want me to bring the money Marco?"

"The airport. Leave now and I'll meet you in the car park. And Donna. Don't you say a word to anyone. Not a word to your daughter or that rabid pig she has in tow. Just quietly leave. You understand? You'll go down with me if you don't do this."

Donna grinned, wondering if she should be ashamed of how much she was enjoying not being intimidated. How much she was enjoying seeing Marco with no power. He still thought he controlled her though. She played along.

"I just need to pack some things," she said. "I'll just pack one—."

"There's no time woman." He was failing miserably to hold on to his temper, and the hysteria in his voice revealed the level of his fear.

"I only got one ticket. There's only one seat left on the first flight out. It's better this way. I'll find us somewhere to stay, and then you can come out later. Nothing will happen to you anyway. You've got them believing it was *my* fucking pot."

"What about Darryl?" she asked. Laurence had told her that Marco hadn't been anywhere near the other crashed vehicles, and wouldn't have any way of knowing whether or not the occupants were dead or alive.

"Stop wasting time talking, and start driving Donna," Marco said. "I'll sort Darryl out. You have absolutely nothing to worry about. He'll get his house. Please."

Laurence's face was red with rage by this time, and his hand kept twitching towards the phone.

"I'm really sorry," she said, feeling calm and strong, and bored with playing this game. "I can't help you."

"What? What are you talking about?" Marco's voice had risen again. "Are you not hearing what I'm saying? There's no choice here. Just get in the damn car and bring that cash to the airport. Do it *now*, or else—. Or—."

"Or else what Marco? What are you going to do to me? Tidge is on his way to the police station right now. He has the phone that you left of the table. You know. The one with the messages from loan sharks and drug dealers on it. When he gets there, he will be informing them that you were found in a vehicle containing enough drugs to put you away for years and years. And also that the people in the vehicles found with yours contained known criminals. An all-points bulletin will be issued, and if you're not already flying out of the country, you'll be stopped before you can leave."

She could hear him breathing heavily, but he said nothing.

"I'll tell you what I'll do," she said. "I'll make sure that your friend gets his money back. I have no use for drug money. And I won't tell anyone where you are or what you're doing. Then you have a fair shot of getting away. Run away Marco, and never come back."

"You ungrateful *bitch*," Marco started. "All the years I—."

"Goodbye Marco," she said. "Goodbye."

She disconnected. They looked at the phone for a while, but it didn't ring again. Laurence laughed.

"Now that took some courage," he said. "Clever of you to let him believe that those criminals are still around. This way you can keep this house, and you'll have more than enough money to live on"

"Yes," she said. "That money is bad karma though. I don't want to keep it for myself."

He nodded. "Let's see what the rest think. I'm sure Elvira will mystically produce a solution to that problem."

*

Laurence went home when the sun came up, and Donna spent the day with Shelley and Tidge. She knew that he knew that there was a lot more to this story than she was sharing, and she was extremely grateful that little more was said about her husband. Apart from her friends calling to see how she was doing, her phone remained silent.

The last thing that Shelley said as she got in the vehicle to leave was, "This time he's gone too far Mom. He won't come back."

"No," said Donna. "I don't think he will. Does that bother you baby? That you might not see your father anytime soon?"

Shelley laughed long and loud.

"Never would be too soon for me Mom. I'm glad he's gone. And I'm glad he can't hurt you anymore."

Donna blinked, wondering how much her daughter had known all along. Shelley said no more on the subject of her father though, just gave her mother the tightest hug, and the promise that they would visit much more often now.

*

Elvira was worried because the old age home was up for sale.

"Whoever buys it could be more hands on than the last lot were," she said. "That would make it really difficult to help the old people. I wish I could buy it with the funds we have in place, but that would pretty much flatten the golden egg as far as monthly interest is concerned, and then we wouldn't be able to buy so many supplies anymore."

Donna hadn't got around yet to telling her friends, all now seated around her kitchen table sipping wine, about the briefcase full of money she had casually deposited under her sink. She looked at Laurence, who was tapping her foot with his. His grin and wiggling eyebrows suggested a solution to the karmicly tainted funds.

Marco had made it to Australia, and phoned her several times, pleading with her to fly out there with the cash, and then sent his ardent wishes that the house burned down with her in it when he finally believed her that she'd returned the money to Darryl because he no longer wanted the house. She told him that all three men had been back several times looking for him, and also that the police were very keen to interview him. And then he stopped calling. As the days went by, and she began to see the world with unfrightened eyes, Donna knew that there was nothing more he could do to her. No matter how hard he tried. And she doubted that he'd try anymore, because she was no longer any use to him. She fetched the briefcase and set it down in the centre of the table before opening it.

"Wow man," said Saul.

Donna laughed, and explained where it had come from. Elvira scowled a little, lost in thought.

"It's tainted alright," said Sandy. "But handing it in won't change what tainted it. I think that helping the old folks might just untaint it though. Drug money buying drugs to help rather than harm."

"Yes," said Elvira, scowling no more. "Of course it will."

Chapter Twenty Two

Donna smiled, watching the old people strolling through her orchards, ripe apples scenting the warm air. She looked at the small Dresden figurines on the table in front of her, and her heart swelled with love for the man who had gone out of his way to find them for her. They weren't the same as the ones she'd lost, but she knew that these that Laurence had bought for her would always be her most treasured possessions. Elvira had bought several old trestle tables and chairs, and the friends had set them up under the trees, and covered them with bright red and white gingham. They were covered with cakes and pastries of all descriptions, bottles of wines and freshly squeezed juices. A day out to celebrate their purchase of Rainbow Acres.

Even though only a few months had passed since Marco had left, and she still was far from healed, she now relished every minute of every day. She knew that she'd had a lucky escape. Not many victims of psychopaths escaped quite as comfortably as she had done. But as Elvira said, she hadn't planned for things to turn out this way. She'd been fully prepared to leave with nothing, but Marco's vicious and selfish attempts to save himself had backfired, and left her with the only things she'd ever loved while with him.

"Divine justice," said Elvira, as if she'd been reading her mind. Donna glanced sharply at her friend, who smiled enigmatically, and raised her glass.

"Here's to the future," she said, winking. "And to twists of fate, and angelic intervention."

"Never mind the witch," said Sandy. "Too much champers I think. But yes. Here's to the future. How are the renovations going Laurence?"

Laurence was sitting as close to Donna as he possibly could, idly bouncing her ankle up and down with his foot.

"Chair lifts are in. Ramps are done. We should be able to start inviting some old folk from the other homes in the district in a month."

With the money in the briefcase not quite spent on the purchase of Rainbow Acres, Laurence had suggested that they turn his family pile into a special care home for the elderly. Not the ones who could afford special care though. Even though their main focus had been on Rainbow Acres, the group also visited the other homes in the district, which were a lot more difficult for their tenants to end their lives in any sort of comfort in, and they'd listed all those who needed their help the most.

"Are you going to stay here?" asked Elvira. "Even if he can't get to you himself, Marco still knows where you are."

Donna shook her head. "No," she said. "I'm going to sell this place and move to Wilson Springs. I love my gardens here, but I don't love the memories of living here."

"Donna's moving into the other cottage at my house," said Laurence with a smile. "She'll be right on site for any potions the old people need, and to generally brighten up my days. And the rest of my life too hopefully."

"Aah," said Elvira, winking at Donna. "I see."

Donna laughed. Elvira might know what the future held, but she didn't want to. For now she was safe and happy, and learning how to live again. Learning how to be loved again.

Recommended Reading

Psychopath Free - Peace

Let Me Reach – Kim Saeed

Malicious Self Love – Sam Vaknin